Durkheim and the Internet

Durkheim and the Internet

Sociolinguistics and the Sociological Imagination

JAN BLOMMAERT

BLOOMSBURY ACADEMIC

LONDON • NEW YORK • OXFORD • NEW DELHI • SYDNEY

BLOOMSBURY ACADEMIC
Bloomsbury Publishing Plc
50 Bedford Square, London, WC1B 3DP, UK
1385 Broadway, New York, NY 10018, USA

BLOOMSBURY, BLOOMSBURY ACADEMIC and the Diana logo are trademarks
of Bloomsbury Publishing Plc

First published in Great Britain 2018

Cover design by Olivia D'Cruz

Library of Congress Cataloging-in-Publication Data
Names: Blommaert, Jan author.
Title: Durkheim and the Internet: on sociolinguistics and the sociological
imagination / Jan Blommaert.
Description: London; New York: Bloomsbury Academic, 2018. | Includes
bibliographical references and index.
Identifiers: LCCN 2017046789 (print) | LCCN 2017050882 (ebook) |
ISBN 9781350055209 (ePub) | ISBN 9781350055216 (ePDF) |
ISBN 9781350055186 (pbk.: alk. paper) |
ISBN 9781350055193 (hardback: alk. paper)
Subjects: LCSH: Sociolinguistics. | Durkheim, âEmile, 1858-1917.
Classification: LCC P40 (ebook) | LCC P40 .B47 2018 (print) |
DDC 306.44–dc23 LC record available at https://lccn.loc.gov/2017046789

ISBN: HB: 978-1-3500-5519-3
PB: 978-1-3500-5518-6
ePDF: 978-1-3500-5521-6
eBook: 978-1-3500-5520-9

Typeset by Deanta Global Publishing Services, Chennai, India
Printed and bound in Great Britain

To find out more about our authors and books visit www.bloomsbury.com
and sign up for our newsletters.

A man with one theory is lost
(Bertolt Brecht)

For Ben Rampton and Rob Moore

CONTENTS

PREFACE

Whenever we do research, we carry along large sets of assumptions, often tacitly and often without much critical reflection. These assumptions are a form of imagination, and they consist of images of social actions and the contexts in which they are situated, all of which we presume to be adequately represented and enacted in the empirical data we examine and, by implication, validating the actual ways we examine such data. Since these sets of assumptions are often shared by large bodies of researchers, they also identify and define disciplines, schools and trends of scholarship – again often tacitly and without being made too often into objects of inquiry in their own right.

In this book, I shall engage with such deeply rooted, widespread and defining assumptions in a very broad field of studies of language-in-society, for which I propose to use the label of 'sociolinguistics' as an ad hoc shorthand, mainly for reasons of editorial parsimony but also for more substantial reasons. My own work over three decades has been performed under a variety of labels, from 'pragmatics' and 'discourse analysis', via 'literacy studies', 'narrative studies', 'linguistic landscape studies', 'social media studies', 'educational linguistics' and 'linguistic ethnography', to 'sociolinguistics' and 'linguistic anthropology' (with an occasional foray into 'linguistics' and 'literary studies'). It was held together, in spite of its diversity, by a central concern about the complex place of language in society, the dialectics that tied language and society together, and the difficulties of decoding, understanding and explaining such ties – a central concern which is fundamentally 'sociolinguistic', if you wish.

My choice of 'sociolinguistic' as the ad hoc label here, therefore, points to the fact that I wish to address assumptions that direct and guide work addressing, in a wide variety of ways, the ties between language and society. And this, of course, makes this a work of theory. But two qualifications are in order.

First qualification: theory, in my view, is in no sense definitive; it is merely an intermediary stage in a longitudinal process of knowledge development. It is a stage where 'the concepts, postulates and premises [are being] straightened out', after which, to quote Gregory Bateson's fine lines,

> analysts will be able to embark on a new and still more fruitful orgy of loose thinking, until they reach a stage at which again the results of their thinking must be strictly conceptualized. (Bateson 1972: 87)

Bateson put a premium on this 'combination of loose and strict thinking' which he saw as 'the most precious tool of science' (1972: 75). Scientists need the messiness and chaos of actual confrontations with empirical cases and data in order to arrive at systematic theories, which then must again be used in 'loose' practices of scientific problem-solving. As for the latter, their very looseness 'allows us to discover phenomena whose existence we were unaware of at the beginning of the research' (Becker et al. 1961: 18). The looseness, thus, enables the critical fact-checking of theories. The theories I shall present here will be most useful if they are used in that sense: as moments of 'strict thinking' in between moments of actual problem-solving which can confirm, defy or amend them. They were not written for eternity.

For this is the second qualification: theory is a tool from and for research. This may sound self-explanatory, but it is not: there is a terrific amount of theory available that is presented as a self-contained intellectual product, to be solely addressed as *theory*. Not here. Whatever theory I have to offer has its feet firmly in very large amounts of empirical research; it represents a moment of 'strict thinking' in an ongoing research process, and it must be fed back to it. Why do we need it then? To quote Anselm Strauss, we need theory to 'stimulate your imagination as well as suggest research directions to you' (Strauss 1993: 50). The imaginative dimension of theory, Strauss argued, can help us

> by enhancing sensitivities to what otherwise might be overlooked; it raises astute questions ... that might not be raised; and it can minimize becoming captive to overly simple explanatory models, or doctrines, that are claimed as interpreting or explaining human life and behavior. (1993: 49)

Rather than constraining thought, I see theory (as understood here) as liberating, as a tool that enables us to explore further and think what has not been thought before. The theories that enable such liberating creativity must naturally be its first victims. But as I said, they were not written for eternity.

The kinds of research on which my theoretical statements are based are sociolinguistic in the sense specified above; the research directions they might suggest, however, are not confined to sociolinguistics but should be influenced by it. In this book, I look at society through the lens of language and interaction; the things we, as sociolinguists, have come to know about how humans interact by means of continuously expanding and changing language-communicative resources, can serve as a take-off point for looking at how society-at-large moves, changes, develops. This is the core assumption in this book: that sociolinguistic insights have far wider relevance, that they constitute a tremendous asset for innovative social thought, and are ready to be deployed in a very wide range of research efforts in social sciences and humanities.

While I have written this book in the strictest solitude and as a process of reflexive critique, it is and remains, of course, the fruit of dialogue – an intense collaborative dialogue I have maintained with a large community of colleagues, research partners and friends. Much of what it contains was raised as a topic of discussion with consecutive generations of PhD researchers – as informal seminars or as direct targeted dialogue on specific analytical issues – and with close colleagues in my own institution, the InCoLaS consortium, and further afield. I avoid listing names here, for the list would be extraordinarily long (and still necessarily incomplete). Many friends, colleagues, partners and students will know that they are included in these opaque lines, and to many others I should say: when in doubt, consider yourself addressed and gratefully acknowledged for the inspiration I received from you.

In a more practical way, this book owes its smooth and painless birth due to Gurdeep Mattu of Bloomsbury, who 'discovered' the draft version and offered me the excellent publishing support of his team, and to my 'executive editor' Karin Berkhout, who, as so often, made sure that a pile of paper turned into a book manuscript. I thank both for their contributions to this project.

Antwerp, June 2017

CHAPTER ONE

Sociolinguists as sociologists

Over two decades ago, the Welsh sociologist Glyn Williams (1992) wrote a devastating review of the sociological underpinnings of the sociolinguistics of his day.[1] His findings were (not to put too fine a point on it) that sociolinguistics was often a combination of very good and even avant-garde linguistics with conventional sociology. So, while sociolinguists appeared as leaders and innovators in the field of advanced linguistic analysis, they would be mere followers in the field of sociological reflection, happy to adopt, often implicitly and without much questioning or motivation, mainstream forms of 'sociological imagination' (cf. Mills 1959). This led to images of society characterized by social integration, social consensus and cooperation, the relative stability of social relations and identities, and clearly delineated national units and group identities as circumscriptions for analysis – recipes from the kitchen of Talcott Parsons, according to Glyn Williams.

It is certainly true that sociolinguists have largely avoided discussing major theoretical issues in sociology and social science, and have been extremely prudent in explaining the big sociological issues that may emerge from their work.[2] This is a great pity, since contemporary sociolinguistic work *does* often yield insights that are challenging mainstream sociological assumptions, and do so at a fundamental level – the level at which, to quote C. Wright Mills (1959: 5), 'the framework of modern society is sought, and within that framework the psychologies of a variety of men and women are formulated', the level, in short, at which we can form a 'sociological re-imagination', a re-imagination of our fundamental conceptions of humans and their social lives. In this text, I intend to undertake a modest attempt in that direction.

The main motive driving this attempt has already been given: contemporary sociolinguistics is sociologically relevant. And the reason behind this can be picked up quickly while reading sociological classics: they invariably refer to patterns of interaction as fundamental to whatever is understood by social relationships, social structure or social process – and usually also grant great importance to this. To quote just one of them, this is how Georg Simmel defined the task of sociology:

> Sociology asks what happens to men and by what rules they behave, not insofar as they unfold their understandable individual existences in their totalities, but insofar as they form groups and *are determined by their group existence because of interaction*. (Simmel 1950: 11, emphasis added)

Yet, with a mere handful of exceptions, they pay hardly any attention to the actual nature and features of such patterns of interaction.[3] Sociolinguists do just that, it is our profession. And systematic attention to communicative modes and processes, we shall see, has the potential to reveal the weakness of certain commonly adopted sociological assumptions and conclusions. It is my conviction that the 'socio' in 'sociolinguistics' involves the responsibility to work from language towards society. What eventually needs to be clarified and explained, through the analysis of sociolinguistic processes, is society and how humans operate in it and construct it. This becomes increasingly pressing as our field of study is changing from 'offline' communication in a precisely circumscribed social space to include rapidly evolving and changing delocalized 'online' communication in superdiverse environments, with well-recorded challenges to established analytical frameworks. I want to encourage my fellow sociolinguists to take that responsibility seriously: we *do* have something to say that transcends the narrow confines of our own field of inquiry, and we should say it. Sociolinguists are, whether they like it or not, specialized sociologists.[4]

In my attempt, I will use Emile Durkheim's work as my point of departure. Why? Not just because of its pervasive influence on Parsons. From reading Durkheim's work, I found that his lasting influence across a broad swath of social and human sciences is often underestimated. It is in his work that the fundamental imagery of Man and society was constructed that became the perimeter, so to speak, within which twentieth-century social thought moved and developed. And even if later scholars dismissed his work or claimed to be free of his influence, they still adopted some of its fundamental principles. We're all, in many and often surprising ways, still Durkheimians.[5] And after extracting some relevant points from Durkheim's work in Chapter 2, I intend to work with Durkheim in two different ways in Chapters 3 and 4.

One, in support of Durkheim, I wish to add to, and refine, a notion he saw as absolutely foundational for sociology as a science: *le fait social*, the social fact. This notion, when Durkheim first formulated it, was highly contested (to the extent that Durkheim spent most of the preface to the second edition of *Les Règles de la Méthode Sociologique* defending and clarifying it; Durkheim [1895] 2010). It was also rejected in what came to be known as Rational Choice Theory and, more generally, it clashed with the tradition of Methodological Individualism. The notion of social fact, of course, determines the possibility of a definition of 'the social' as a sphere of phenomena and processes that cannot be reduced to constituent parts without losing much of their essence. Thus, it also underlies the very possibility of a sociology and a sociolinguistics. A highly precise and analytically powerful view of the social fact is possible if we excerpt some advanced sociolinguistic work, which I shall argue in Chapter 3.

Two, we need also to step away from Durkheim and the world he tried to make sense of and consider our own. There are things now that Durkheim could not possibly have known or predicted, and contemporary sociolinguistic work on internet phenomena raises several entirely new fundamental questions about the nature of social groups, social relations and social processes and permits new hypotheses in these domains. By combining this second exercise with the first one, we arrive in Chapter 4 at a number of fundamental propositions – at theory, in other words – that may contribute to work in several other disciplines, and that have been generated inductively by detailed empirical attention to the facts of language, interaction, communication, of which we know that they are absolutely central to any social phenomenon. Or at least: let's try to establish that.[6]

Notes

1 In this text, I shall use the term 'sociolinguistics' as a broadly descriptive umbrella term including any approach in which the connections between language and society are systematically explored and in which communication is seen as an *activity* not reducible to the production of cognitive content. Work to be discussed in what follows might, consequently, more conventionally be labelled as linguistic anthropology, pragmatics, applied linguistics, discourse analysis and so forth – and disciplinary sociolinguistics.

2 There are some notable exceptions; see, for example, Fairclough 1992; Chouliaraki and Fairclough 1999; Coupland 2016; Flores, Spotti and Garcia 2017; Perez-Milans 2017.

3 Some of the exceptions are reviewed in John B. Thompson's (1984) *Studies in the Theory of Ideology* – most prominently Bourdieu, Habermas and Giddens. Thompson himself, of course, also ranks among the exceptions (see especially Thompson 1984, 1990).

4 Some would say: microsociologists. But for reasons that have to do with the very nature of language, to be discussed at length in

what follows, I tend to have strong reservations regarding that facile micro/macro dichotomy. See Collins (1981) for a discussion and Collins and Blot (2003) for a very fine illustration of why sociolinguists are not necessarily just microsociologists.

5 I do not suggest here that we are *only* Durkheimians: we are also, equally unwittingly, Weberians, Marxians and Freudians for instance. I choose Durkheim as a point of reference because some of the fundamental concepts he designed are highly useful in the particular exercise I shall undertake here. And as a gesture to express that, sociolinguistics, as I see it, has some things to say on fundamental sociological and social-theoretical questions.

6 Throughout this attempt, I will follow Garfinkel's understanding of Durkheim (shared by several others) as concerned with empirical detail rather than conceptual generalization, and with what Durkheim called 'the objective reality of social facts' as something that can be demonstrated by attending to concrete, situated and embodied instances of social (inter-) action (see e.g. Garfinkel 2002). There are, therefore, aspects of Durkheim's work that I shall not mention and discussions on the interpretation of his work that I shall not involve myself in, for I do not need all of Durkheim's work nor any interpretation of it in order to make the points I intend to make.

CHAPTER TWO

Durkheim's social fact

Emile Durkheim devoted his life to the self-conscious construction of sociology as a science, and by the end of his life, he had achieved that goal. In his view, scientific sociology was a necessity in *fin de siècle* France. Durkheim shared the widespread sense of discomfort of his compatriots, epitomized in the military defeat against German forces in 1870, which led both to the end of the second Empire and to the revolution of the Paris Commune. Society-as-we-knew-it appeared to be falling apart. People had become weak, decadent, hedonistic and individualistic, and a generation-long process of industrialization, with the growth of a large urban proletariat in mushrooming cities, had disrupted France's national sociocultural cohesion, and hence had prejudiced its future as a strong nation. Sociology, for Durkheim, was one of the tools needed to reconstruct a sense of membership among the French, of a community that was characterized by specific and exceptional features – to be discovered by scientific sociology and to be spread by a new system of 'moral education' (the title of his celebrated course of lectures; Durkheim [1961] 2002). This sociology was, thus, *aspirational* and *prescriptive*, a sort of 'ortho-sociology'; rather than just describing what was there, Durkheim set out to convert factual description into normative prescription in view of constructing a society that, in his understanding, was not yet there.[1]

2.1 Norms and concepts

This normative-prescriptive aspect is a point we need to remember, for it explains the particular focus of Durkheim's sociology, *norms*; or to be more precise: the secular moral order that should characterize the rational, industrial and science-based French society of the Third Republic. The existence of such an order – implicit and often invisible in everyday life – was what Durkheim posited as 'the social fact' that made his sociology possible; and the vigorous promotion, spread and enforcement of this order was the nation-building task of the modern French state, via its education system. Eventually, this rational civic moral order should replace religion as the belief system underlying and organizing society, becoming as 'sacred' as, previously, religious beliefs. The latter were, according to Durkheim, veiled and misconceived understandings of the real, essential moral order:

> We must discover those moral forces that men, down to the present time, have conceived of only under the form of religious allegories. We must disengage them from their symbols, present them in their rational nakedness, so to speak, and find a way to make the child feel their reality without recourse to any mythological intermediary. (Durkheim [1961] 2002: 11).

Durkheim's analogy of the secular moral order with the moral order propagated in religion would, in later stages of his career, push him towards profound engagements with religion as a social fact. For in both the secular and the religious moral order he saw the same features at work: both were experienced and perceived as beyond the grasp and intention of individuals, and as compelling norms of social life. In the case of religion, they emanated from a divine force; in the case of social facts, society provided them; in both cases, individuals acquired them through extended interaction in their communities as well as through institutionalized forms of learning and education.

These features, then, formed the definition of his 'social fact'. Social facts are forms of behaviour and thought that are (1) 'exterior to the individual' and (2) experienced by individuals as coercive, constraining and imperative rules, deviation of which would come at a price (see e.g. Durkheim [1895] 2010: 100; discussion in Lukes 1973: 8–15). They are, in short, *collective rules* of which individuals are (at least intuitively) aware and to which they *must* submit. Here is one of the many formulations provided by Durkheim:

> A rule is not then a simple matter of habitual behavior; it is a way of acting that we do not feel free to alter according to taste. It is in some measure – and to the same extent that it is a rule – beyond personal preference. There is in it something that resists us, is beyond us. (Durkheim [1961] 2002: 28)

The religious analogies are plain: the social order is sacred in Durkheim's eyes. The social fact, thus defined, was the object of Durkheim's new sociology; the defining characteristics of social facts should distinguish the new discipline from psychology (a science devoted to *individual* behaviour and thought). Durkheim soberly observed that people act differently when they are alone from when they are in the company of others. When alone, instincts, pre-social desires, would regulate behaviour (and would be the terrain of psychological analysis); social behaviour, by contrast, was regulated by 'collective conscience' – what we could now call an 'ideology' – and by a moral discipline pushing individuals to bring the extremes of their instincts under control so as to be acceptable in the eyes of others.[2] In that sense, the development of social behaviour marks a transition from 'absolute existence' (humans in their natural state) to 'relative existence' (humans in relation to others and to institutions), from an a-moral state to a moral state, and from a mode of solitary autarky to one of solidarity and labour division (cf. Lukes 1973: 125; many of these notions were already elaborated in Durkheim's dissertation, *De la Division du Travail Social*, [1893] 1967).

The collective conscience, note, is made up of 'collective representations' – things we would now call 'concepts', relatively fixed meaning frames. And while institutions such as state-sponsored education transmit, across generations, certain collective representations typical of the nation-state, such representations are acquired alongside more specific ones characterizing and organizing life in particular social groups (caste, class, family, profession, etc.). The norms that organize social life are, in other words, layered and scaled. Socialization proceeded both at the level of becoming a citizen of a (homogeneous) country and at the level of becoming a member of (more diverse) specific social sub-groups. The function of both is the same: norms always presuppose 'a certain disposition in the individual for a regular existence – a preference for regularity' (Durkheim [1961] 2002: 34). Social rules are, simply put, 'limits to our natural inclinations' (ibid.: 96).

Now, although Durkheim would underscore the fact that 'man always lives in the midst of many groups', his views on which specific groups we should think about differ from publication to publication, and even when he mentions groups he does not necessarily devote much analysis to them. *Moral Education* specifies just three such groups: the family, the nation (or political group) and humanity ([1961] 2002: 73–4), for instance, and only the nation is elaborately discussed – not surprising in a book that aspired to reorganize national education in France. Elsewhere, he would profoundly examine professional groups and religious groups as well. In all, Durkheim had a strong preference for what we could call 'thick' groups, groups in which people shared *a lot* of norms, values and collective representations, and as we shall see later, his influence has been pervasive in that respect.

2.2 Integration and anomie

Let us recall Durkheim's motives for the development of a sociology. He was gravely concerned about the perceived loss of sociocultural cohesion in the France of his day. He believed he was witnessing the disintegration of an old social order, while a new one was not yet in place. Consequently, his sociology consistently addressed issues of sociocultural cohesion or integration: how did this rapidly changing society maintain a reasonable degree of cohesion? In *De la Division du Travail Social*, he pointed towards one answer: new forms of solidarity grounded in the emergence of new, smaller, professional groups were complementing older forms of solidarity grounded in 'deep' sociocultural ties. And they did so by developing alternative moral orders and collective representations – the defining features of the 'social' as we have seen earlier, and in that sense also the defining features of identifiable social groups. Members were integrated into such groups by subscribing to and adopting these defining features, by 'enregistering' (we would now say) the moral codes that shaped such groups and held them together. In other words, integration is a factor of successful socialization of individuals into the moral orders of social groups, and social cohesion is an aggregate of such forms of integration.

One of the most interesting and productive concepts developed by Durkheim is that of *anomie*. Anomie describes a situation in which individuals reject available normative orders or cannot draw on them, either by absence of such orders or because access to them is restricted. Anomie stands for 'normlessness'. Durkheim discussed the concept elaborately in his *Suicide* ([1897] 1951), and he did so from the viewpoint of social cohesion. In a rapidly changing society where an old order is on its way out while a new order is under construction, he argued, numbers of people find themselves in a moral no man's land where the rules of the social game are unknown, unclear or in need of development. Anomie, we could say, is the concrete face of social disintegration and individual marginalization. And Durkheim saw his own rapidly transforming society as prone to anomie, with individuals at risk of being poorly or incompletely socialized and at a loss finding out what it takes to do well. This moral no man's land explained the high statistical incidence of suicide, and Durkheim provided a primarily *social* explanation for suicide.

With some qualifications, Durkheim saw anomie as something negative, a lack of a clear and widely shared moral social order; individuals caught in anomie are marginalized, deviants, outsiders. At the same time, he saw anomie as an inevitable feature of sociohistorical change and, in that sense, as a constant feature of societies at any point in time. A fully integrated society was an aspiration rather than a reality, and at any moment in their historical development, societies would be characterized by old and new normative systems coexisting in sometimes uncomfortable ways. Durkheim did not see the creative and productive potential of anomie – the ways in which anomie spawns alternative ways of social organization. His view of anomie can also be made more useful when it is understood not as a top-down phenomenon – from the 'centre' of society towards its margins – but as a general relational phenomenon operating at all levels of social life in the form of (negative) normative judgements of one about another. The margins of society, seen from this more broadly scoped view, are spaces where alternative social orders are quite rigorously observed and policed – as Howard Becker (1963) famously demonstrated.

2.3 Durkheim's impact and the challenge of Rational Choice

I have deliberately been selective here, focusing on elements from Durkheim's work that offer immediate possibilities for critical re-evaluation in view of sociolinguistic evidence. Let me summarize and reformulate these elements in a series of related propositions.

1 There is a set of human forms of behaviour that are collective, in the sense that they cannot be reduced to individual agency or intention. They are acquired socially, through socialization and education processes,

in a variety of groups. They have a sui generis reality which cannot be explained by explaining individuals' enactments.

2 These forms of behaviour must be seen as governed by sets of sanctioned norms, or ideologies, and the character of these norms is moral. Social behaviour is moral-normative.

3 These sets of norms characterize social groups, notably 'thick' groups such as those of the nation, class, caste, family, profession, religion. We always live in a plurality of such groups.

4 These sets of norms are the key to social cohesion and integration: people who submit to them will be perceived as 'normal' members of their social groups, while people deviating from them will be confronted by anomie and risk becoming outcasts.

In a variety of formulations, these four propositions can be found throughout twentieth-century sociology (and beyond). Durkheim's sociology was, like that of for example Dewey and Bourdieu but unlike that of for example Weber (Gerth and Mills 1970: 58) first and foremost a sociology of *communities* and of *social cohesion*, and it opened several areas of exploration that became foundational for twentieth-century social sciences. These areas included the study of ethnoclassification and ethnoscience (through his work with Marcel Mauss), collective memory (through his student Maurice Halbwachs), labour organization and labour institutions (influencing, to name just a few, Everett C. Hughes, Herbert Blumer and John Kenneth Galbraith), socialization (influencing e.g. Jean Piaget), religion, cultural symbols and ritual (influencing e.g. Victor Turner and Erving Goffman) and several others.

It was Talcott Parsons who turned the priorities of Durkheim's programme into the systematic theory to which Glyn Williams took exception, in the effort significantly simplifying some of the most interesting but often unstable aspects of Durkheim's work – notably the relationship between 'society' and 'social groups' and the place of individual agency in society.[3] Parson's sociology, as we know, focused on integration at the level of 'society' (e.g. Parsons 2007). Societies would remain integrated because of the widespread acceptance of specific and relatively enduring sets of *values*, while *norms* characterized smaller social groups. Norms could differ from the dominant values, of course; they could even run counter to these values, but they were distinctly 'lighter' than values.[4] Thus, in a text written in 1964 on US youth culture (at that time perceived as rebellious and increasingly deviant), Parsons confidently concluded that

> American society in a sense appears to be running its course. We find no cogent evidence of a major change in the essential patterns of its governing values. (Parsons 1964: 181)

In other words, the long-haired, pot-smoking and anti-Vietnam young rebels of the early 1960s were still good and decent Americans, and their shocking behaviour did not shake the foundations of the American mode of integration. Four years later, such an argument would prove to be hard to sustain, and not just in the United States (Elbaum 2002).[5]

As I said above, Durkheim was very much a sociologist of communities, of the collective dimension of social life. The most radical challenge to this came from what is now known as Rational Choice (Theory) (Green and Shapiro 1994; Adamae 2003). Rational Choice is an outgrowth of Methodological Individualism, something Max Weber introduced as a doctrine in the social sciences (and was taken further by e.g. Hayek and Popper). Simply put, Methodological Individualism is the theory complex in which every human activity is *in fine* reduced to individual interests, intentions, motives, concerns and decisions, because (it is argued) individual levels of subjectivity in action (even if eminently social) are the only ones available to the analyst (Heath 2015).

Rational Choice is a radicalization of the 'individualism' in Methodological Individualism. Human action, in Rational Choice, is driven by one motive, the maximization of individual 'profit' (material as well as symbolic), and it proceeds by means of calculated, intentional and rational decisions by individuals ('choice'). Since Durkheim's moral order crucially depended on the suppression (or 'moderation') of individual interests and preferences – egoism is typically seen as immoral – the theoretical dichotomy could not be sharper.[6]

Rational choice, in that sense, is a fundamental denial of Durkheim's 'social fact'. Even more: it is a lock-stock-and-barrel denial of the entire Durkheimian sociological imagination, for 'there is no such thing as society' (to quote Margaret Thatcher's slogan). In Kenneth Arrow's (1951) famous view, any form of collective (rational) choice is just impossible. Arrow, 'proved' this in his so-called 'Impossibility Theorem', quite incredibly by means of intricate mathematical argument – and mathematics reshaped (and replaced) field-observation-based sociology as the privileged source of knowledge on humans and their social practices (Adamae 2003: 102–16; cf. Blommaert 2016a). To the disbelief of empirical sociologists such as Everett C. Hughes, if certain social practices were ruled mathematically impossible, it was assumed that their occurrence in the real world was exceptional or accidental (cf. Hughes [1971] 2009: xix, 348–54).

Rational Choice never made a real inroad into sociolinguistics; but it largely dominates several social-scientific and humanities disciplines, most notably economics (cf. Thaler 2015).[7] Revisiting and revising Durkheim's social fact from the perspective of contemporary sociolinguistics – the exercise I shall embark on in the next chapter – therefore implies a rejection of Rational Choice. A good reason for this is that in the more radical varieties of Rational Choice, people never seem to communicate, or they communicate only in dyadic logical argument when they are allowed to.

Notes

1 Observe that Durkheim, although generally seen as a conservative thinker, was not a reactionary. The society he

wished to help construct was a *new* one, not a (mythical) older society that needed to be preserved or recovered. Durkheim saw the present as unstable and unreliable, an old world that had vanished while a new one had not yet taken solid form and was moving in negative and destructive directions. His rejection – a moral rejection – of the present is quite radical, and contrasts remarkably with that of his contemporary Simmel, who viewed similar tendencies with a neutral, nonjudgemental gaze, as a challenge rather than as a problem.

2 This insistence on temperance and moderation, often presented as evidence of his politically conservative and bourgeois views, can also be seen as another feature of his analogy between secular and (Christian and Jewish) religious moral systems. Foucault (2015: 240) concludes his course on *The Punitive Society* with this caustic remark: '[Power] is hidden as power and passes for society. Society, Durkheim said, is the system of the disciplines, but what he did not say is that this system must be analyzed within strategies specific to a system of power.' Foucault saw the normative-disciplinary complex emerging in the nineteenth century as a core feature of the developing capitalist mode of production, and Durkheim's work on the division of labour as a codification of this process, in which he 'normalized' a system of power specific to and instrumental for this new mode of production.

3 See Parsons (1937). Parsons was not alone in seeking completion of the Durkheimian project. To name one already mentioned, it is hard not to see Foucault's sustained effort to describe and delineate the emergence of the modern 'normal' individual through forms of discipline as an idiosyncratic engagement with some of Durkheim's unfinished business. See, for example, Foucault (2003, 2015). Likewise, one can profitably read, for example, Bourdieu's *Distinction* (1984) as an elaborate engagement with Durkheim's notions of social cohesion and anomie.

4 Much of the pioneering literature on 'late' or 'Post'-Modernity implicitly takes this Durkheimian-Parsonian integrated society as its benchmark. Thus, for example, Zygmunt Bauman's 'liquid modernity' evidently takes a 'solid modernity' as its point of departure (Bauman 2007). Whether such a solid modernity was ever a reality rather than a projection of a

specific sociological imagination remains an untestable research question, although works such as E. P. Thompson's *The Making of the English Working Class* (1968) strongly suggest that the degree of integration of our societies in an earlier stage of their development may have been grossly overrated.

5 Needless to say, Parsons' view of US society as integrated was fundamentally challenged, and some will say shattered, by Gunnar Myrdal's monumental *American Dilemma* (1944).

6 Judging from Durkheim's ([1897] 1951) discussion of 'egoistic suicide', egoism is, in effect, a killer rather than a cornerstone of social conduct.

7 The few attempts to use Rational Choice in sociolinguistic work were rather epic failures in social analysis. Carol Myers-Scotton's *Social Motivations for Codeswitching* (1993) used an awkward conception of Rights-and-Obligations sets attached to 'codes', from which speakers would rationally choose the most advantageous one; the actual social settings in which code-switching occurs were dismissed as accidental, not fundamental (see Meeuwis and Blommaert 1994 for an elaborate critique); in David Laitin's *Language Repertoires and State Construction in Africa* (1992), an equally awkward variety of Game Theory is used to arrive at an ideal, rational '3 + 1 language outcome' for language policy in Africa. The argument is entirely detached from anything that ties languages to real social environments.

CHAPTER THREE

Sociolinguistics and the social fact: *Avec* Durkheim

So let us first establish this: people *do* communicate; they communicate all the time, in highly diverse and complex modes, often with more than one interlocutor, and not always logically, economically or rationally; it is through interaction that they are recognized as 'social', as a 'subject', and as producers of ideas. Affirming this is, of course, of an extraordinary triviality. But this *trivium* has been denied and neglected in tons of sociological and other social-scientific work, turning it not in a truism but into a hard-fought methodological principle. Establishing that principle means affirming the very possibility of a *socio*linguistics. And I think we have pretty decent empirical back-up for this principle and, thence, for the possibility of sociolinguistics. So let us show some of that evidence in what follows.

I repeat what I mentioned earlier: while almost every major sociologist would emphasize (or at least mention) interaction as a given, detailed attention to interaction has never really been part of the sociological mainstream. Interaction was paid lip service to, and communication is often seen as a set of rudimentary transmission practices not worthy of study in its own right – something so elementary that it belongs to the décor in which real social action is played out and does not demand further examination.[1] Blumer, defining the methodological position of symbolic interactionism as it was being kept in the margins of the sociology of his time, lamented (1969: 7):

> A society consists of individuals interacting with one another. The activities of the members occur predominantly in response to one another or in relation to one another. Even though this is recognized almost universally in definitions of human society, social interaction is usually taken for granted and treated as having little, if any, significance in its own right.

Durkheim was no exception. And this, remarkably, led to generations of sociologists overlooking what is potentially the most self-evident social fact. Let me sketch some aspects of it, and start with the most general one.

3.1 Language as a normative collective system: Ordered indexicality

People can only communicate with others when they share and deploy different forms of 'grammar' – conventionalized normative patterns *ordering* the potential mess of symbols we call language, ensuring that we 'make sense' to each other. This simple observation should be sufficient to establish it as a Durkheimian social fact *pur sang*.[2] But let me elaborate this – begging the reader for tolerance for the highly sketchy summary of complex histories of linguistic thought in what follows.

The different forms of grammar can – roughly – be divided into grammars of form and grammars of usage, and usually the term 'grammar' is reserved for the former: the fact that the formal, morphosyntactic organization of linguistic expressions is governed by language-specific (i.e. non-individual) rules, compliance with which displays some degree of flexibility but is overall quite strict and relatively stable and enduring.

Description of these formal rules became 'linguistics', and their relatively stable and enduring character became the key element in identifying separate 'languages' (cf. Silverstein 1977; Irvine 2001; Bauman and Briggs 2003; Blommaert 2013; see Agha 2007a: 222 for a concise discussion). As for grammars of usage, they gradually became a separate domain of study (called 'Pragmatics') through the work of language philosophers such as Austin (1962), Grice (1975) and Searle (1969) (cf. Verschueren 1999). Here, too, relatively stable and enduring rules were detected, although the overlap between such rules and separate 'languages' was less outspoken. Rules of politeness, for instance, appeared to be connected more to social and cultural groups than to the actual 'languages' they use, and were even seen as potentially universal (Brown and Levinson 1987; for a critical appraisal see Eelen 2001). A generation of anthropologists had, in the meantime, provided mountains of literature on the sociocultural embedding of language in specific (often 'ethnic' or 'tribal') communities (see Hymes1964 for a survey), while symbolic-interactionist sociologists in the United States had started exploring the social-scientific significance of everyday patterns of social interaction in their own social environments (e.g. Goffman 1959; Garfinkel 1967; Blumer 1969).

The eminently social fact of grammar, remarkably, became individualized as soon as *universals* became the ambition of linguistic theory, in the wake of Noam Chomsky's epochal reformulation of linguistic as a science of 'competence' – the mentally structured capacity to generate grammatically well-formed sentences (e.g. Chomsky 1965). Chomsky announced that the focus on competence meant that linguists should be concerned with an 'ideal' speaker/hearer operating outside of any form of real communicative situation; and this ideal speaker became an *individual* speaker whose 'language' existed, in universal ways and (contrary to De Saussure's view) perfectly, in his or her individual brain (see Katz 1972 for an excellent example and Cicourel 1973, Chapters 3 and 4, for a critique). Methodological Individualism, thus, entered the science of language through the detour of psychologism, and social and cultural norms were replaced by mental operations unaffected by (socially and culturally contextualized) 'performance'. Language had become an a-social fact.

Modern sociolinguistics was a reaction to that; and from its very beginnings, work in sociolinguistics would struggle to re-establish language as a social fact. Reaching back to the oeuvres of Sapir and Whorf, the abstract language designated as the object of linguistics was countered by situated, contextualized 'speech' and such speech had to be understood in terms of a dialectics of language and social life, lodged in a 'speech community' (Hymes 1966, 1972, 1980; Gumperz 1968, 1982). And apart from a (possibly) mentally hardwired and universal grammatical competence – the *linguistic* system – one should also consider the group-specific and culturally relative communicative competence – the *sociolinguistic* system (Hymes 1992). Communicative competence, note, referred to knowledge of the sociocultural norms of language and the capacity to deploy them adequately in a variety of social circumstances. The norms of language, thus, were defined as sociocultural constructs in a theoretical frame emphasizing action; and Michael Silverstein (again drawing on Whorf) put a gloss on them: 'language ideologies' (Silverstein 1979).

I shall be forgiven for this breathless rush through half a century of intellectual development, for I have arrived now where I wanted to arrive. The concept of language ideologies, which rose to prominence and became a unifying focus in the 1990s (Kroskrity, Schieffelin and Woolard 1992; see Blommaert 2006a for a review), offered a comprehensive framework for revisiting language as a social fact, in nearly all aspects. The central idea proved extraordinarily productive: language is used on the basis of socioculturally grounded conventions dialogically organizing its production and understanding; the empirical basis for such ideologies are concrete 'indexicals', that is features of communicative action pointing in nonrandom ways to salient, context-specific sociocultural meaning reservoirs, and ultimately to social structure (see Agha 2007b;

also De Fina, Schiffrin and Bamberg 2006; Cicourel 1973 and Gumperz 1982 can be seen as precursors). Indexicals, thus, invoke conventionalized and therefore presupposed histories of meaningful usage (or 'models', Gal 2016: 119) and precipitate them into new moments of deployment with active, responsive interlocutors. In Silverstein's words:

> Now any indexical process, wherein signs point to a presupposed context in which they occur (i.e. have occurred) or to an entailed potential context in which they occur (i.e. will have occurred), depends on some metapragmatic function to achieve a measure of determinacy. It turns out that the crucial position of ideologies of semiosis is in constituting such a mediating metapragmatics, giving parties an idea of determinate contextualization for indexicals, presupposable as shared according to interested positions or perspectives to follow upon some social fact like group membership, condition in society, achieved commonality of interests, etc. Ideology construes indexicality. In so doing ideology inevitably biases its metapragmatic 'take' so as to create another potential order of effective indexicality that bears what we can appreciate sometimes as a truly ironic relation to the first (1992: 315).

This principle could be applied to the formal grammar of language, which appears subject to strong language-ideological effects (e.g. Silverstein 1979; Errington 1988; Irvine and Gal 2000); to the learning of language norms in socialization processes (e.g. Schieffelin and Ochs 1986); to the use of specific 'registers' governing concrete sociocultural domains of speech and subject to processes of incorporation called 'enregisterment' (e.g. Agha 2005, 2007b); to patterns of everyday narratives (De Fina, Schiffrin and Bamberg 2006); to lay and institutionalized concepts of language, including sociolinguistic hierarchies and attributed speaker identities (e.g. Silverstein 1996, 1998; Agha 2003) and the politics of language at nation-state level and in more specific institutional contexts (e.g. Jaffe 1999; Blommaert 1999; Philips 2000; Haviland 2003); to intertextual processes of meaning-making, resemiotization and entextualization (e.g. Silverstein and Urban 1996); to complex contemporary forms of meaning- and identity-making involving codeswitching (e.g. Rampton 1995, 2006). En route, a large number of crucial concepts in the study of language were redefined: language itself, speech community, genre, style (Gal 2016) and so forth: the range of themes, concepts and domains that were profoundly reshaped by the conceptual development of language ideologies is extensive.

The truly fundamental theoretical and methodological impact of language ideologies, in view of the exercise I undertake here, is that it has given us an extraordinarily precise view of norms (and their cognates 'values' and 'collective representations'). Norms, we now see, are language-ideological phenomena produced and enacted in communicative action. They are, more precisely, *ordered indexicalities*: sets of indexicals organized in relation to each other, with some of them being 'emblematic' of the meaning effects they generate – a sort of register 'shibboleth' effect, as when someone starts a sentence with 'oh dear' versus 'fuck' (cf. Silverstein 2003; Agha 2005, 2007b; Blommaert 2005), or shifts into a mock accent so as to project an evaluated identity on someone else (e.g. Hill 2001; Rampton 2006). The fundamentally normative, dialogical and interpreted character of social relations, thus, becomes clear: whenever we interact with others, we produce not just the kinds of denotational meanings one finds in a dictionary, but we produce *evaluative* meanings, in which the words, actions and identities of all the participants are weighed and given (sociocultural) value. And in so doing we produce, moment by moment, 'culture' and 'society', as well as 'identity' and 'meaning'. None of these concepts can be detached from interaction – 'language *and* culture', for instance, have merged into the interactional production of indexical order (Silverstein 2004).

Echoes of Bakhtin and Goffman are evident here: language ideologies can in many ways be seen as an extreme

methodological refinement of the general ideas articulated by
Bakhtin (1981, 1986) and Goffman (1971, 1974). Bakhtin's
sociohistorical theory of literary form has now been extended
into the entire field of language in society, and has acquired
far more analytical purchase and precision; while the micro-
orders of social conduct described by Goffman can now also
be reformulated in a more systematic and generalizable way.
I shall come back to the continued relevance of both authors
further on; in the case of Goffman, we shall see that, in a wider
sense, the programme of symbolic interactionism (and to some
extent, of ethnomethodology) is coming back with a vengeance
(cf. Blumer 1969; Cicourel 1973; Garfinkel 2002). In addition,
and combining Bakhtin with Goffman, ordered indexicalities
presuppose, and necessitate, a *dialogical* and *intersubjective*
conception of meaning-making that stretches over the entire
range of behaviours deployed in what we call 'interaction' or
'communication'. Whenever we communicate, we keep an
eye on the other and adjust our communicative behaviour
to an anticipated uptake from our interlocutors. In contrast
to what Rational Choice suggest, we are quite altruistic and
cooperative in communication, and we are happy and eager
to accommodate the other in our own language use – as
demonstrated whenever we revert to a kind of pidgin English
when an obviously confused tourist ask us for directions. Our
communicative behaviour is regulated by the fact that it is
organized together with others.[3]

Three final remarks are in order.

1 Orders of indexicality are obviously collective, social
phenomena. I have qualified them as 'nonrandom' on
a couple of occasions already, and this is vital because
any form of understanding requires recognizability
in terms of a *specific* set of ordered indexicals. An
interaction opened with 'excuse me, sir' versus one
opened with 'hey, you!' is likely to be a different
interaction (probably a difference glossed as 'polite'
versus 'impolite'), and recognition of this difference can

only occur when the participants share the language-ideological valuations of these indexicals. And they do. A study by Silverstein (2015) on public (online) discussions of New York accent showed remarkable similarities in several categories of valuations given by participants, something that corroborates Penelope Eckert's (2008, 2012) notion of 'indexical fields'. Linguistic variation, it now appears, is subject to powerful collective language-ideological forces ('We have come to see variation as a more robust and dynamic indexical system' – Eckert 2015: 43; also Rampton 2006, 2016a). Section 3.2 will return to this.

2   People display an outspoken tendency to *create* norms whenever they are absent or unclearly scripted, and new communication technologies provide us with plenty of examples of that. The extremely rapid development of new social media platforms and apps, one can say, presents their users with a situation of anomie each time they engage with such novelties. And whereas common wisdom would often qualify mobile phone texting codes and Facebook interactions as 'anything goes' because the carefully indoctrinated school standards of language and script appear to be violated continuously, a more concentrated analysis shows that even such apparently open, highly diverse, free and unscripted communicative spaces are very rapidly filled with ad hoc (and rapidly solidified) norms, defining modes of interaction, genres and styles, and subject to sometimes rigorous policing. These new norms can and do function as tools for evading or subverting imposed, top-down rules when existing rules are experienced as oppressive (e.g. Varis and Wang 2011; Wang, Juffermans and Du 2012; Blommaert 2012; Leppänen and Elo 2016; Du 2016; Stæhr 2017). As said before, anomie may be defined

as a space without norms; at the same time, it is also
a space where *new* norms are invited, demanded and
manufactured – a creative space in which 'the social',
as grounded in the sharedness of sets of norms, is
instantly shaped. To rephrase this with reference to
Rational Choice: we see in this phenomenon of instant,
grassroots norm-creation how people continuously
surrender their individual choice and freedom to joint
patterns of regulation and policing. Because they do
not want to get stuck talking to just themselves, one
can imagine.

3 While ordered indexicals organize and generate
'meaning', such meanings are not just 'rational', that
is denotational, but also, and simultaneously, aesthetic
and dramatic. In fact, when people communicate, they
perform a bundle of functions: epistemic, affective,
poetic, performative (Hymes 1980; Haviland 1989;
Bauman and Briggs 1990). And it is this bundle – not
just its epistemic aspect – that turns communication
into something that satisfies higher-order social and
cultural demands (Hymes 1966, 1996; Silverstein
1985, 1997, 2004; Blommaert 2006b, 2015c). We
convince others not just by the pureness and truth-
conditional excellence of our argument, but even
more by the stylistic-narrative performance in which
it is cast and by the evaluative key in which we frame
it; and we pay meticulous attention to all of this
while we build our argument. In the view of Charles
Goodwin (2007), there is something inherently moral
in epistemic practices, since the latter demand a tightly
organized set of moves within a chosen participant
framework, rupture of which is seen as a moral as
well as an epistemic issue (cf. also Goodwin 1994).
This simple observation blows out of the water any
theory in which human communication is reduced
to the rational exchange of pure (and perfectly

retrievable) meanings. To put it somewhat crudely
and in folksy terms: human rationality is very much
tied up with, in practice even indistinguishable from,
human *ir*rationality – emotion, morality and aesthetics.
We are very subjective when we believe we are
objective and can get quite emotional when we discuss
'the facts'.[4]

I have used a lot of space discussing this first element –
language as a normative collective system, now understood
through the conceptual instruments of language ideologies –
for it underlies several of the points that follow. I can treat
these points somewhat more concisely now.

3.2 Language variation: Dialects, accents and languaging

I have already mentioned above (pace Eckert) that language
variation is now seen as an indexical system of distinction.
Language is the great diversifier: even the smallest feature
can serve as an emblem of fundamental identity difference
(Rampton 1995; Blommaert 2015b). But let us start where we
have to start: with the features that index such distinctions,
language variation itself.

Recall the elements that Durkheim identified as defining the
social fact: social facts (a) were phenomena that transcended the
control of the individual and (b) had a compelling, normative
effect on individuals. Now consider a straightforward case:
all over the world, people learn a language we call English;
they do so, in formal education, on the basis of a corpus of
teaching materials that are amazingly similar (in fact, they can
be seen as standardized industrial mass products). Yet all over
the world, and in spite of the near-uniform input, people speak
English *with an accent*. These accents are clearly identifiable:
few would not be able to tell the difference between, say, an
'American' accent and a 'French' one, and many would be

able to distinguish an 'Indian' accent from a 'Nigerian' one. In fact, such distinctions have led to the development of a branch of applied linguistics called 'World Englishes' (e.g. Bhatt 2001; also Pennycook 2007; Seargeant 2009; Mufwene 2010), where different regional realizations of English are no longer seen as deviations from 'standard' English but as bona fide language varieties in their own right, often with names such as 'Hinglish' (Hindi-English: Kothari and Snell 2011) or more generically 'country name + English', as in 'Brunei English'. The range of 'typical' features, for instance in Brunei English, is extensive and stretches from phonetics and morphosyntax into discursive and lexical differences. The explanations for such differences are usually sought in influences from language contact with 'native' language substrates, the specific history of English in the region, the local or regional language policies and the education system (Deterding and Sharbawi 2013). In the case of Hinglish, apart from these factors, the influence and prestige of a powerful Hindi-language popular culture is also noted (Kothari 2011). (Observe that we are addressing a globalization phenomenon here, and I shall return to this.)

The fact, however, remains the same. People growing up and living in specific regions of the world acquire features of speech that are distinctly, and identifiably, regional – 'from there'. These features – accents – are extraordinarily powerful identity shibboleths; in fact the word 'shibboleth' itself refers to a biblical story in which accent in speech was used to distinguish allies from enemies (and to kill the latter, appropriately identified). And getting rid of an acquired accent is quite a slow, difficult and sometimes painful job, for which, in the meantime, a branch of specialized therapists and providers has emerged (cf. Blommaert 2008a; Silverstein 2015). Variation in speech, we can see, is not something one typically chooses – it is acquired through socialization processes, that is through a shared history in a community in which the fine distinctions of speech are learned and embodied. Those are phenomena that transcend the individual, no one really *owns* them.

As for their compelling, normative effects, we must keep earlier remarks in mind and turn to a venerable branch of sociolinguistics: social dialectology in the tradition of Peter Trudgill.[5] Drawing on Britain and Cheshire (2003a), several points are worth noting.

1 *Collective identity* appears to be the main driver guiding the dynamics of dialect. More specifically, dialect, however defined, is a shibboleth for regional identity, that is a recognizable identity shared by people inhabiting a particular region, currently or in the past; dialect indexes the local and the regional (also Johnstone 2010; Silverstein 2015).

2 Identity issues also govern innovation and change. The latter depend strongly on *degrees of social integration*. The better people are integrated in the community, the more they will contribute to innovation in dialect, due to the tendency to index specific sub-groups within that community. Social isolation – as with for example spatially isolated 'outliers' in poorly populated areas – slows down the patterns of change in dialects (Britain 2003).

3 'Dialect levelling' – a well-known feature in dialectology, in which dialects appear to develop in a more convergent way, depends on social factors as well: *speech accommodation* between speakers of different dialectal backgrounds (Kerswill 2003).

4 The tendency to index specific subgroups through dialect innovation highlights (a) the heterogeneity of dialect 'speech communities' and (b) the importance of 'loose social networks' (Watts 2003; also Silverstein 2016) in language change.

5 Throughout all of the above, 'social categories are … seen as ideologically-driven processes' (Britain and Cheshire 2003b: 4): the dynamics of dialect change is governed by language-ideological attributions –

the normative and identity-projecting phenomena discussed in the previous section (also Rampton 2009; Gal 2016).

The latter can be observed in yet another dimension of language change: *languaging*, the extraordinarily creative mixing and blending of linguistic and expressive resources typical of sociolinguistically highly complex environments (Jørgensen 2008; Creese and Blackledge 2010; Jørgensen et al. 2016; Juffermans 2015; Madsen, Karrebæk and Møller 2015; Blommaert and Rampton 2016). While languaging, at first sight, appears like unregulated bricolage or mash-up business or a kind of communicative anomie (and is often so perceived by those in charge of guarding the gates of language correctness), a closer look reveals a tremendous level of structuring, all of it governed language-ideologically by delicate shifts in (identity) 'footing', alignment between speakers and changes in the participant framework. Needless to say that current social media usage displays a phenomenal amount of such forms of languaging in new forms of graphic practice (e.g. Tagliamonte 2015; Du 2016).

The bricolage can, in effect, reveal differences between locally constructed and discernible varieties (Kailoglou 2015; Madsen 2017; also Rampton 2011), and can be a powerful instrument for 'styling' specific identities – ironically, ritually, playfully, or quite seriously (Rampton 1995, 2006; Coupland2007, 2015; Cutler 2009). The more serious forms of styling may revolve around highly ritualized minimal displays of a 'heritage language', with tremendous identity-establishing effects (e.g. Moore 2017). And 'quite seriously' can also mean 'making money', of course: the commodification of language variation in new economic sectors – think of tourism, marketing and call centres as examples – has turned sociolinguistics into the profitable exchange of more than just symbolic capital (Heller 2010; Jaworski and Thurlow 2010; Blommaert 2010; Kelly-Holmes 2010; Woydack 2017).

3.3 Inequality, voice, repertoire

In discussing languaging, I have already pointed to the linguistic and expressive resources that people use in such complex forms of discursive work. Such resources are, of course, not evenly distributed in any society, and the reasons for this are social.[6] Hymes (1996: 26–7) stated this problem clearly: while language obviously offers a pool of opportunities to people, it simultaneously acts as a *constraint*; it is a human social treasure trove as well as a human social problem, since no single person knows all of a language, and meeting the limits of what we can communicate is an acutely frustrating social experience for all of us. Throughout life, we continuously acquire new sets of resources while we shed older, obsolete ones; and in its most general sense, we are always constrained by what is communicable and what is not – we often have no words for what needs to be expressed.[7] But let me focus on two specific elements by way of illustration: (1) access to specific register and genre resources and (2) access to specific contexts for communication.

1 In general, and contrary to the suggestion of the ideal (or 'native') speaker/hearer, no real human being has access to all the resources that circulate socially, for several reasons. There can be institutional barriers reserving 'elite' resources for a small group of people, creating effective hierarchical patterns of access to what Bourdieu (1982) called 'legitimate language' – and access to 'standard' English in large parts of the world is a case in point (Park and Wee 2012; Blommaert 2010, 2014). People have easy access to spoken vernacular varieties of English widespread in global popular culture and open to informal learning – which is why words such as 'fuck' and 'shit' occur almost everywhere – while literacy-based standard varieties are far more difficult (and expensive) to obtain, and specialized registers such as legal-bureaucratic,

literary or academic varieties even more so, since they demand access to effectively policed formal learning channels and 'members only' communities of users. Thus, illiterate people are likely never to produce written discourse, and not because of choice but because of social-institutional structural reasons. And there are many misunderstandings that are grounded not in an individual's poor choice of words but in an asymmetrical degree of communicative competence between speakers (Gumperz 1982 is a classic; also Roberts 2016). Processes of access restriction are not necessarily 'institutional' though: similar forms of gatekeeping occur almost everywhere. Howard Becker's (1963) *Outsiders* described how 'marginal' social groups such as marihuana-smoking jazz musicians also deploy tactics of selection and exclusion through specific modes of talk distinguishing 'those in the know' from newcomers or ignorant 'outsiders'. Much of the literature on styling and languaging reviewed earlier addresses exactly such small peer-group identity dynamics in which group-specific, exclusive, enregistered phonological, morphosyntactic, lexical and genre features are made emblematic of membership and eligibility (cf. Silverstein 2006; Blackledge and Creese 2016).

2 As to restrictions of access to specific contexts, again, nobody has access to all available contexts that make up the communicative economies of societies. This is again clearest in institutional contexts, where, for instance, defendants and witnesses in courts have no access to the context of verdict-making, which is exclusively reserved for the judges. More generally, expert contexts are often decisive in social life, while they are tightly controlled on a 'members only' basis by the experts themselves (e.g. Cicourel 1967; Briggs 1997, 2005; Mehan 1996).

We often have no impact on what others do with
our words in patterns of re-entextualization we call
'text trajectories', in which a subject's statement
is recorded by someone, summarized in a report
by someone else for yet someone else, who takes a
decision which is then moved down the trajectory
and fed back to the subject – as in bureaucratic
procedures or newspaper interviews (e.g. Blommaert
2001). Obviously, access to such restricted contexts is
already conditioned by (1) above: one needs specific
forms of language and literacy proficiency in order
to enter such social spaces. And in a world in which
large chunks of communication demand access to
hi-tech ICT equipment and infrastructures, such
inequalities display no tendencies to disappear (Wang
et al. 2014).

Both forms of inequality would operate across the spectre
of the sociolinguistic system, but of course, some would be
subject to more outspoken and structural forms of exclusion
and marginalization than others. Hymes himself focused on
the predicament of Native American groups, and speakers
of small, minority or immigrant languages are, evidently, in
structurally weaker positions than speakers of majority and
prestigious varieties – recent sociolinguistics has provided an
avalanche of work on these themes (for an elaborate case study,
see the essays in Blommaert et al. 2012). Thus, sociolinguistic
inequalities characterize every social system, and the causes
for such inequalities are social. Hymes (1996) coined the term
'voice' for the actual capacity of people to make themselves
understood and noted that problems of voice represent the
critical dimension of sociolinguistic work: rather than merely
describing sociolinguistic diversity as a kind of juxtaposition of
equally valuable varieties, we should engage with the question
as to why particular varieties are, in actual fact, not equal to
others – questions of voice as a sociopolitical given, voice as
the reflection of social structures in the actual communicative

abilities of people (cf. Blommaert 2005, 2008b; Van der Aa 2012; Scott 2013).

The latter move involves and presupposes attention to *repertoires*: the actual resources people have acquired and can effectively deploy in communication. The notion of repertoire has only recently been made into a topic of profound reflection, often from an awareness that widespread qualifications such as 'speaker of language X', or even '*(non)native* speaker of language X' are entirely inadequate as descriptors of the tremendous diversity in degrees of proficiency and communicative ability people display (e.g. Blommaert and Backus 2013; Rymes 2014; Busch 2015). Repertoires are by definition uniquely individual and can be described as 'indexical biographies' reflecting the social experiences of people with specific orders of indexicality – exposure, immersion, learning, informal acquisition – and the ways in which such experiences reflect the social order and inscribe individuals into a wide variety of group memberships. What is in people's repertoires is usually there for a good reason: because they needed it at some point in social life. In that sense, repertoires are traces of social norms, or if you wish, traces of the compelling and often even coercive and consequential evaluative responses of others in our lives – traces of power, in short. Taking that to the theoretical level: repertoires once more show how becoming and being a unique individual is a fundamentally social process – socialized, dialogical, normative, dynamic.

Facts of sociolinguistic distribution, we can see, shape a field of power and are reproduced by it, and turn language, in its various manifestations, into a heavily policed object in which potentially every difference can be turned into a consequential form of inequality. The term 'voice', as used here, points towards this consequentiality: the normative organization of language – notably the tendency to standardize forms of language and language usage into highly politically sensitive templates – affects the life chances of people, and sociolinguistics has brought a wealth of evidence to this point. Specifically through the lens of sociolinguistic analysis, we can observe in great detail the way in which an infinitely fractal system of normativity – indexicals and their forms of order – turns into a capillary power structure in Foucault's (2015) sense, with on the one end elaborate formal and institutional systems of 'language testing' (e.g. Extra, Spotti and Van Avermaet 2011; Spotti 2016),[8] and on the other end the minute-by-minute evaluative judgements of people's communicative actions by their interlocutors in everyday life.

3.4 Language, the social fact

If Durkheim would have attended more closely to language and how it operates in and through society, he would have had considerably less trouble establishing his *fait social*. Half a century of sociolinguistics has proven, at great length and in infinite detail, that language can *only* be explained as a social fact – other explanations are absurd. Particularly absurd, we can conclude quite confidently, is Rational Choice. Almost everything that has been brought up by sociolinguists flatly contradicts the central assumptions of Rational Choice and offers loads of hard and conclusive empirical evidence for this contradiction. The worldview of Rational Choice, from a sociolinguistic viewpoint, is that of a world populated by people who only talk to themselves.

Perhaps the greatest advantage of sociolinguistics, and its most important contribution to sociological theory, is the highly detailed and precise view of *normativity* I discussed in Section 3.1. The 'norms', 'values' and 'collective representations' that characterize the Durkheimian (and Parsonian) assumptions about integration and social coherence are given a feet-on-the-ground realism as continuously evolving, dialogically constructed social actions in which meaning, in the traditional linguistic sense, is entirely blended with sociocultural, intersubjective evaluations of a moral nature, precipitating what we call 'identity'. Identity is not a product, nor an *a priori*, but the material of interaction itself and, so, the material of social order. Since this material is extremely diverse, the social order is too, and the robust confidence with which, for instance, Parsons (2007) spoke about the 'American core values' appears entirely unjustified from the viewpoint of sociolinguistic evidence – the price of analytical precision is ontological diversification (Parkin 2016).

Remember that one of the central arguments in favour of Methodological Individualism was that in human action, only *individual* subjectivity was observable. On the basis of what we have seen so far, this argument, too, has been dealt a death blow. One of sociolinguistics' contributions to a theory of social action is *inter*subjectivity: the fact that people, when communicating, require a dialogically established normative template shared with others in order to arrive at 'meaning'; the latter is an interpretive effect, constantly negotiated and accommodated intersubjectively (and not necessarily by means of 'purely' rational means). To the extent that social action is communicative action, it is *joint* action (cf. Blumer 1969; Cicourel 1973).

In the next chapter, I shall add to what has been established so far. There were things that Durkheim and his successors in the Grand Tradition of sociology could not possibly have known. They nuance some of the assumptions underlying classical sociology and they open exciting alternative trajectories of sociological re-imagination.

Notes

1   The assumption seems to be: since we all do it, there is no need to study it. Hence Hymes's critical views of the communication-focused work of Bourdieu and Habermas – two exceptions to the rule just sketched here (Hymes 1996: 52–6). My own verdict on Bourdieu is significantly more merciful (Blommaert 2015a). As for Habermas's *Theory of Communicative* Action, (Habermas 1984), I share Hymes's critique. Hymes points to the abstract and normative-idealized treatment of communication patterns

in the work of both, detecting a lack of sensitivity to the actual ways in which language functions in real social environments. Habermas can be said, at most, to specify a set of ideal normative *preconditions* for communication.

2 De Saussure, who attended lectures by Durkheim, already pointed to 'a grammatical system that exists virtually in every brain, or more precisely in the brains of a community of individuals; because language is never complete in any individual, it exists in its perfect state only in the masses' (1960: 30; French original, my translation). Observe here how De Saussure adopts Durkheim's concept of 'social fact' and, as we shall see, deviates strongly in this from the Methodological Individualism characterizing many subsequent developments in linguistics.

3 I cannot enter into detail here, but the well-known Gricean Maxims (Grice 1975) assume cooperativity in communication as a given – in general, we want to understand and be understood whenever we communicate – and there is an entire tradition of 'Accommodation Theory' in which speech convergence between interlocutors is studied (Giles, Coupland and Coupland 1991). Cooperation is also the central assumption to most of Conversation Analysis (e.g. Schegloff, Jefferson and Sacks 1977).

4 Knowledge practices in science are no exception, and there is a large methodological literature criticizing the claims to objectivity made in various branches of science. Aaron Cicourel's *Method and Measurement in Sociology* (1964) famously confronted mainstream statistical research with the problems of inevitable subjectivity in interaction. His critique had a profound effect on Bourdieu's methodology as well, and for Bourdieu, the only possible road to objectivity was the recognition of subjectivity in knowledge construction (Blommaert 2015a; for a cognate argument see Fabian 1983).

5 Note that 'dialect' in the traditional sense is a notion that has come under fire from language-ideologically inspired linguistic anthropology. Gal (2016: 117) observes that varieties defined on the basis of situation of use – 'registers' – are hard to distinguish from those associated with spatial identity – 'dialects' and 'sociolects'; Silverstein (2016) adds to this a historical reanalysis showing how traditional dialect research can, and should, be reformulated as concerned with enregisterment. This idea was a central assumption in Agha (2007b) as well.

6   Without too much comment, I can observe that this view
    obviously clashes with the notion of the 'ideal speaker/hearer'
    that became the hallmark of Chomskyan linguistics (see section
    3.1 above). What follows can be read as a straightforward
    empirical refutation of this notion.
7   Foucault (1969) coined the term 'archive' to identify the limits
    of what can be conventionally thought and understandably
    communicated: if we communicate within the archive, we are
    'normal' and others will understand us; if we communicate
    outside the boundaries of the archive, chances are that others
    will qualify us as lunatics. See Blommaert (2005: 99–103) for a
    discussion.
8   Many of these forms of language testing could doubtless be
    categorized as forms of 'power without knowledge', to use
    David Graeber's terms, 'where coercion and paperwork largely
    substituted for the need for understanding … subjects' (2015: 65;
    see also Section 4.8). The benchmarks of such testing modes are
    usually fictitious 'standard' forms of language, imagined levels of
    competence, and ludicrous projections of degrees of fluency onto
    broader sociopolitical levels of citizenship. This form of science
    fiction, nonetheless, has become increasingly prominent as an
    instrument of power and exclusion in the field of migration,
    almost everywhere.

CHAPTER FOUR

What Durkheim could not have known: *Après* Durkheim

Several of the phenomena discussed in the previous section bore the imprint of globalization. An acute awareness of globalization as an ongoing reality-shaping and reshaping process is what sets our sociological imagination apart from that of Durkheim and his followers, who operated within the confines of the nineteenth- and twentieth-century nation-state and its social and institutional organization. Durkheim was, along with many of his disciples, a methodological nationalist whose sociology did accept change (indeed, as we have seen, coming to terms with social change was what prompted Durkheim to his intellectual efforts), but change within a sedentary system which was coincident with the nation-state. This is remarkable, for globalization was very much a reality in Durkheim's days. Colonization and an increasingly integrated world economy – Hobsbawm's '*Age of Empire*' – had brought the world to places such as Paris and London. But this world was seen through the spectre of one's country, the structures, needs and imagination of which depended, precisely and paradoxically, on its global reach.

The current phase of globalization is, on the one hand, qualitatively different from that of the Age of Empire, and this is to a very significant extent an effect of the internet – a technology that changed the world in the last decade of the twentieth century, allowing a tremendous increase in speed, volume and density of global flows and networks (see Castells 1996; Eriksen 2001). Due to this change, Hobsbawm (2008: 155) observes how 'the Empire expands wider still and wider': the global internet infrastructure and the pattern of traffic density mirrors, astonishingly, global information networks established in the late nineteenth century; persistent global inequalities are, in that sense, extended and expanded by the internet (see Read 1992; Blommaert 2016b). And such processes shape as well as occur in a new environment of communication and information, the details of which we are beginning to understand (cf. Seargeant and Tagg 2014; Varis and van Nuenen 2017). The point in all of this is that those who prefer to believe that there is nothing fundamentally new to the current stage of globalization are quite dramatically wrong. We are indeed witnessing a very, very profound qualitative change with momentous effects on the nature and circulation of knowledge and sociocultural norms, as well as on the structure of communities and social cohesion. More on this below.[1]

But on the other hand, as said earlier: perhaps even more importantly, the present stage of globalization is accompanied by an *awareness* of it, an awareness that social processes nowadays operate at a variety of scales, of which the nation-state is just one and the global reach of the World Wide Web another. And this awareness is *revisionist* in nature, as it forces us to revisit and redirect a sociological imagination circumscribed and coloured by methodological nationalism. Both points – a qualitative difference and a different awareness of globalization – are things that did not belong to the worldview within which Durkheim and his successors such as Parsons operated.

In what follows, I shall explore the revisionist effects of this. And I shall do this by proposing a series of theories emerging from contemporary sociolinguistic work. I shall be using a simple assumption: if interaction is what makes us social, theoretical insights into interaction must have wider relevance and can be used as a template for theorization at a higher level.[2] As noted at the very beginning, formulating theories is not exactly sociolinguists' bread and butter – but the editor of a recent volume on theoretical debates in sociolinguistics explicitly invites it (Coupland 2016). So let me try.

It goes without saying that much of what I shall present here cannot, strictly speaking, be called 'new' theory. Similar ideas have circulated throughout the twentieth century and have gained currency in the first decade of the twenty-first – echoes from Goffman, Giddens, Simmel and even Husserl will be heard, and I took my prompt to engage with these issues from Manuel Castells's (1996, 2010) and Arjun Appadurai's (1996) amazingly accurate (and continuously updated) late-twentieth-century predictions. What sociolinguistics contributes, however, is a set of empirical arguments that make such theoretical propositions compelling and inevitable; it also offers an empirically solid basis for *reformulations* of social theory. Note that while the previous chapter was largely retrospective, drawing on achievements from sociolinguistic research of the past decades, this chapter will be more prospective, drawing on current ongoing work, and therefore also programmatic in tone.

Since the discourse will change, it may not be a bad idea to specify what I understand by the term 'theory'. Theory is a particular kind of statement: a statement that tries to describe and define a *type* of phenomena out there, in such a way that research on individual tokens of these phenomena can be hypothetically generalized in a systematic way. Theories, then, are statements that enable a generalizable heuristics based on hypothesized type-token relationships. Such statements are, ideally and in the tradition of Anselm Strauss's 'Grounded Theory', already saturated with evidence – they are, to some extent, already proven: it is 'theory from data' (Glaser and Strauss 1999: 1; cf. Holton 2008). But even if a theory is already backed up by a serious amount of supporting evidence, in each new piece of research it must operate as a *question* to be answered – or, to use a more familiar terminology, as a working hypothesis. The grounded theories I shall propose are conceptually relatively 'light', for they offer conceptual outlines of broad types of social phenomena to be 'filled in' with empirical detail in actual research.

Finally, I must return to what I said about theory in the preface: theory is not definitive and is made from and for research. I find no better statement to summarize this view than this one:

> In my reading of science, theories arise from the study of events: They vary in scope and abstractness; they are provisional, incomplete, require verification and qualification; they have a life of potential usefulness but having contributed to the movement of a science they vanish or become incorporated in newer theories. (Strauss 1993: 1)

What follows is nothing more than that, and nothing less.

4.1 Preliminary: Vernacular globalization

As I said, I took my prompt from Castells and Appadurai, and I will use a particular notion developed by the latter as a general frame, a 'folder', so to speak, for the theories I shall propose below.

There has been no shortage of globalization theories over the past couple of decades, and some of them are good. But sociolinguistics brings something exceptional to the field of globalization studies: a perspective in which the 'big' movements in globalization (often called 'flows': Appadurai 1996) need to be constantly checked by the minutiae of on-the-ground communicative practices in which such global forces are being enacted and turned into locally performed meaning (see e.g. Pennycook 2007, 2010) – something for which

Appadurai coined the term 'vernacular globalization' (1996: 10). Observe that, for Appadurai, vernacular globalization is more than just a descriptive term, it is a gloss for the general condition of contemporary modernity:[3]

> The megarhetoric of developmental modernization ... in many countries is still with us. But it is often punctuated, interrogated, and domesticated by the micronarratives of film, television, music and other expressive forms, which allow modernization to be rewritten more as vernacular globalization and less as a concession to large-scale national and international policies. (Appadurai 1996: 10)

To be sure, the dialectic of global and local forces in the experiential life-world of human beings (in other words, of vernacularization) is perhaps the most complicated descriptive and methodological issue in the study of globalization processes, and the introduction of a new generation of electronic media has certainly complicated matters. This was noticed early enough. Appadurai (1996: 194) noted 'new forms of disjuncture between spatial and virtual neighborhoods' as an effect of the globalization of new electronic media, seriously complicating the actual meaning of a term such as 'local practice'; he also saw the emerging of 'diasporic public spheres' revealing new horizons for political and social action, previously imagined within the confines of the nation-state (1996: 22).[4] Manuel Castells (1996), in turn, described the massive effect of new information technologies on economic and political processes, on the organization of labour, on identity work and on social organization. Castells predicted the development of a new type of social formation which he called 'network' and which was not contained by the traditional boundaries of social groups. Both (and many more) saw a complex new sociocultural, political and economic order in the making, and invited others to join them in describing and theorizing these changes. Some of those who felt addressed by this call were sociolinguists.

It is my thesis that contemporary sociolinguistics has almost comprehensively theorized vernacular globalization as a condition of everyday life, the outlines of which can be sketched by the keywords *polycentricity*, *mobility* and *complexity*, which also count as its ontological assumptions.

Polycentricity stands for the fact that in every environment for social action, multiple sets of norms will be simultaneously present, although they might not be of the same order – they are scaled, stratified, and in that sense never ideologically neutral even if represented as such (Carr and Lempert 2016: 3). Polycentricity defines the intrinsic *indeterminacy* of social actions and processes, and their *non-unified character*: social change involves parts of society developing faster than others, creating anachronistic gaps.

Mobility is shorthand for the assumption that social life, even if 'local' in so many senses of the word, is never sedentary but always moving from one set of chronotopes into another one, across scales and centres of normative focus (cf. Blommaert 2015d). Mobility defines the intrinsic *instability* of social action and processes.

Complexity makes us aware of the fact that, even if every form of social activity evolves within a *system* of such activities, that system is always unfinished, dynamic and nonlinear or stochastic in the sense that outcomes may not be predicted from initial conditions (cf. Blommaert 2016c). Complexity defines the intrinsic *tentativeness* and potential *redefinability* of social action and processes.

This is, of course, a mere sketch of a theory framework, which in essence represents a cumulative and generalized result of a wide variety of different more precise sociolinguistic theorizations. This theory of vernacular globalization, therefore, requires several other more specific theories, providing more clarity to the keywords. I shall now turn to these more specific theories.

4.2 An indexical-polynomic theory of social norms

Let us recall the insistence, throughout the Durkheimian tradition of sociology, on norms as the key to defining and understanding the social fact, and let us now return to the discussion in Section 3.1 on ordered indexicality. In that earlier discussion, I explained how norms, in contemporary sociolinguistics, need to be seen as nonrandomly organized patterns of indexical order, and I stressed the collective and dialogical character of such sociolinguistic norms as a decisive argument against Rational Choice.

This is an ontological statement, and I believe we can broaden its scope from interaction and its ordered indexicals to social behaviour in general. Seen from that angle, social norms are, in actual fact, *ordered sets of interactionally ratified behavioural details* which we can call *behavioural scripts*. Note, once more,

1 that whatever is normative in social life is socially co-constructed in the process of interactional meaning-making, subject to continuous ratification by others, and therefore *tentative* in character, and

2 that there is nothing abstract to norms (or 'values') other than the terms we use to describe them. In real social life, norms take on a variety of *concrete behavioural shapes*.[5]

But that is not all there is to be said on this, certainly when we consider globalization and its sociolinguistic impact. In order to establish that, let us have a look at some research.

In a truly brilliant study, Sabrina Billings (2014) examined beauty pageants in Tanzania – an outlier, so to speak, in the world of English and of global mediascapes in Appadurai's (1996: 33) terms. Billings focused on how the selection of the most appropriate candidate for Miss Tanzania (through a scaled procedure starting locally, then regionally, then nationally) invoked and deployed sociolinguistic hierarchies in which 'good English' – fluent performance in a variety of English judged to be not-too-local – was the pinnacle of eligibility, even when, officially, candidates could produce public discourse in both Swahili (the national language) and English. Why is 'good English' so important? Because it serves as a crucial indexical suggesting superiority on at least two levels: (1) nationally and due to the particular sociolinguistic history of Tanzania, English is the prestige code associated with the status of being 'educated' (Billings 2014: 38–53); (2) internationally, because national pageant organizers operate within the Miss World format (Billings 2014: 61) and the Tanzanian winner will proceed to the global competition – where 'good English', once again, is a powerful diacritic.

'Good English', as a diacritic in the pageant, is of course not sufficient. The young women competing for the title of Miss Tanzania must also be judged to be physically beautiful, elegant and intelligent (Billings 2014: 92–6). We see a behavioural script emerge here, in which discursive normativity – speaking 'good English'– is an element of the total order of indexicality that rules the pageant. But while it is not sufficient, 'good English' is *decisive*. In several examples, quite painful to read, Billings shows how even top contenders can be mercilessly sanctioned by the critical audience when their on-stage discursive performance in English is judged to be inadequate. Describing audience reactions in one such case, Billings writes:

> The pageant-savvy audience sees through her flimsy effort to insert a memorized response to a different question into the answer slot. In attempting to present herself as a fluent speaker of standard English, the contestant has instead, through her inability to answer spontaneously, indexed herself as a linguistic phony. (Billings 2014: 107)

The candidate's discursive performance, in other words, was judged to be dishonest, and therefore a betrayal of the behavioural script she tried to produce – that of someone who is educated and smart (hence using 'good English') and worthy of proceeding to the Miss World election. Her discursive performance exposed her, in short, as a liar, and this was grounds for exclusion. Norms, we can see once more, have effective power effects.

Note two important points here.

1 We see that the ratification of the failed behavioural script is a judgement of the entire person, and the judgement is moral in tone and character: the candidate is dismissed because her sociolinguistic features were judged to be 'untrue', not authentic, not honest. We see that, in actual practice, the social norms of the Durkheimian world are *moralized behavioural scripts*. Note that the moral, pace Durkheim, is entirely concrete and empirical here, operating on a range of very concrete behavioural features.

2 We also see how such judgements are *scaled*, with at last three different sets of criteria playing into each other in a mutually reinforcing way. There are the national and international indexical orders already mentioned above, and there is the order of the situated, actual moment of performance. The candidate stumbled over words, tried to start again, manifestly repeated an earlier statement and produced a distinct local accent in one expression – and all of this provoked cruel laughter from the audience. Into the perceived violation of local rules of performance, the national and international ones were infused by means of what Irvine and Gal (2000) called 'fractal recursivity', jointly and simultaneously resulting in a shattering disqualification of the candidate.

This is where we can become more precise with respect to the notion of polycentricity mentioned in Section 4.1. Speech events such as the ones described by Billings are governed by various sets of norms operating on various 'dimensions of social life' (Carr and Lempert 2016) and orienting towards different real or imagined centres of authority (Silverstein 1998; Blommaert 2005: 172). Some of these norms are general – think of the norms governing genres such as public speech – while others will be specific – the norms of public speech in a beauty contest in Tanzania, for instance. We can see how this contributes to the theorizing of vernacular globalization sketched earlier.[6]

Furthermore, I believe we can generalize this insight, certainly in the age of widespread social media usage. Communicative actions will always be subject to various simultaneously operating sets of norms, since they will always demand attendance to the rules of actual interactional conduct, those of the topic of the interaction, its purpose or function, the social and cultural conventions governing conduct within specific participant frameworks, particular spaces or times, specific types of encounters, and so forth. A Facebook update, for instance, demands attendance to the (highly dynamic) norms of literacy and linguistic codes, the genre and register norms of an 'update' (not too long, preferably multimodal, etc.), the tacit norms of one's community of 'friends' regarding certain topics and ways to discuss them (think of prevalent political orientations in one's Facebook community), the Facebook rules of conduct (proscribing certain forms of obscenity, for instance), and the rules of the algorithmic system behind Facebook that render certain updates more visible than others. And whether or not one is aware of these rules doesn't really matter: every update will generate *effects* related to all these different but simultaneously operating sets of norms.

Thus, whenever we interact with others we find ourselves in a *polynomic* social arena. We respond not just to one set of norms but to multiple sets of finely defined norms governing aspects of the specific interactional events and its context. We can call such sets of highly specific norms *microhegemonies* – more on this below. And the presence of multiple microhegemonies turns every instance of social action into a polynomic social event.

Sociolinguistic work brings a far more precise and empirically verifiable theory of norms and normativity to social thought than most other approaches. When we think of norms, we see *a polynomic complex of moralized behavioural scripts*: several concrete sets of ordered indexicals microhegemonically governing aspects of conduct, played out simultaneously towards, and with, interlocutors who continuously valuate them morally and feed these valuations back to us. Given the centrality of norms in any sociological imagination since Durkheim, this theory will have repercussions on others.

4.3 A genre theory of social action

The theory of norms I sketched here is a building block of a theory of action: we can now assume that social action is normatively organized in the sense just described. But we have to take this somewhat further, towards a theory of action proper. There is nothing unusual about this. Models for understanding the nature and dynamics of social action have been and remain key ingredients of sociological theorizing in the Grand Tradition, from Weber and Parsons to Bourdieu, Habermas and Giddens, to name just a few. Given my intention to use sociolinguistic insights in interaction as the core of theorizing, symbolic interactionism was obviously a source of inspiration, and I will repeatedly draw on Strauss's (1993) very rich discussion of this tradition of social thought.

Recalling the discussion in the previous chapters, one fundamental assumption I borrow from that source is straightforward: 'Actions are in effect *interactions* between and among group members, not simply an individual's actions or acts' (Strauss 1993: 21, italics in original). Social action, in other words, is a verb. It is collective, is intersubjective, and involves orientations to norms; the concept of 'genre' can be a useful tool for capturing most of this in a very simple way.

Sociolinguistics has for decades been concerned with the notion of genre, as a historically established and socialized set of linguistic-communicative features that enables specific forms of communicative behaviour to be recognized as, for instance, a joke, a lecture, a confession, a poem, a novel (Halliday 1978; Hymes 1981; Bakhtin 1986; Fabian 1991; Blommaert 2008c). From such evidence, we also know that *all* communicative behaviour is genred – or at least, that if we intend to make our communicative behaviour understood by others, it needs to be recognizable as an instance of a specific genre. Genre, thus, operates very much in the sense specified above: while every instance is unique and special, recognizability is *generic*, that is it rests on the iterativity of the ordered indexicals pointing to specific genres. Every novel is recognizable as 'a novel', but still we have our favourite novels.

This insight can be generalized. Social actions do not emerge from nowhere, nor can they be seen as pure acts of creativity. They are performances based on already existing sociocultural material, always uniquely contextualized and situated, and therefore involving a degree of creativity. So two dimensions are crucial here, for jointly they construct social actions as situated, performative genre work:

1 *Iterativity*: the usage of already existing genre templates
2 *Creativity*: the deviation from such templates in unique instances of genre performance

Iterativity provides what we can call the 'structural' aspect of social action. It ensures the recognizability of actions: they proceed largely within existing orders of indexicality that are interactionally understandable-as-something. Generic iterativity also turns situated social action into a fundamentally *historical* phenomenon – where does this iterated sociocultural material come from? How did it acquire its function as generic template? And thereby, of course, it should be seen as a crucial element in explaining sociocultural transmission, reproduction and spread.

Creativity provides what we can call the 'diversity' aspect of social action. It ensures the uniqueness of the situated deployment and performance of genred features of action, of its participants, and of its chronotopic peculiarities – how and why does this particular situated instance of social action function in this particular way? Creativity, in that sense, can be seen as an 'inflection' of genre templates, as a term covering the small bits of deviation-from-a-model that turn the actual instance into something that triggers interactional uptake and appraisal. *This particular* lecture is nice, engaging and fun, versus boring, silly and uninteresting. It is still a lecture – the genre template has been satisfied – but it is a particular evaluated token of that type. Creativity, I add, is also the *aspirational* dimension of social action: the things we want to invent, or attempt to change, by small deviations from the normative templates. And while creativity usually only accounts for a relatively minor part of social action – it is an inflection of iterative templates – in everyday lived experience it prevails over the iterative basis of action. Our reactions and judgements of approval or rejection are based on the inflection, the 'accent', present in the uniquely performed act – which we can judge and react to because it is not entirely unique.

Thus, we can see any concrete social action as proceeding along lines of established normativity and deviations from such norms, as *genred* modes of collective conduct in which the sharedness of what makes actions recognizable is played off against the uniqueness of what is created by deviations from what is commonly shared. Needless to say that longitudinally, creative aspects of action may become iterative ones – exceptions become rules when they have been made into commonly ratified innovations.

There is a strong tendency (and theoretical habit) to see social action as singular, linear and goal-directed; Rational Choice, of course, takes this to its limits. This does not work.

1 Sociolinguistic studies of interaction have shown that actions are best seen as part of longer and more complex sequences, in various ways (see e.g. Wortham and Reyes 2015). One, there is the intertextual nature of interaction, which aligns with the iterative aspect of social action. Actions are meaningful because they can be understood in relation to earlier similar ones (and projected onto future ones) (cf. Silverstein 2005; Silverstein and Urban 1996). Two, what looks like one singular and coherent action may, upon closer inspection, prove to be an array of different overlapping but disjoined actions – and we get changeable constellations of genres-within-genres. A conversation may contain, for instance, moments of intimate narration, of disengaged small talk and of hostile cross-questioning (cf. Goffman 1981); and narratives done in, for instance, police or immigration interviews may simultaneously be recorded into legally consequential textual reporting formats – while the interviewer's on-the-spot interactional routines would suggest nothing more than constructive conversational involvement, he or she might simultaneously be performing a procedural 'next step' practice very much detached from what goes on between the interlocutors during the interview (cf. Briggs 1997; Blommaert 2005). Actions are rarely singular.

2   They are rarely linear as well. The creativity dimension of action also accounts for its contingent nature (in the sense of Garfinkel 1967): the inevitable indeterminacy, open-endedness and uncertainty characterizing any form of social action and manifesting itself in the very well-known category of phenomena we call misunderstanding. Certainly when we consider the earlier point, about actions rarely being singular, we should assume that we often face what Anselm Strauss called 'a cumulative mess': 'an evolving set of problems that are so unanticipated, difficult, and in extreme cases so "fateful" that control of the course of action is threatened and even rendered virtually impossible' (1993: 53). The normal course of

action is often disrupted (a lecture, for instance, by a beeping smartphone), the opening strategy rarely followed through (other than in apocryphal meeting reports), and people whom we believe to thoroughly know can still surprise us. Our interactions proceed in complex, layered contexts and in relation to (often changeable arrays of) other people, which renders their course uncertain and highly dependent on a wide range of factors, only part of which are within our conscious control.[7]

3 The latter has an effect on the question of the goal-directedness of action. Conditions and effects are rarely cleanly aligned, and nonlinear outcomes of interaction are legion – think of people falling in love, or of people entering as friends and leaving as enemies. And while we may have a rational interest in mind when engaging in forms of interaction – think of employment as the rational interest one may have in a job interview – we can be quite irrational in interactional proceedings and depend as much on tacit emotively given-off and picked-up cues as on tightly argued moves – such that we may leave a job interview without the job but with a good feeling. We are ready to adjust our logic to that of the interlocutors and redefine the appropriate interactional features as well as the desired outcomes of interaction in trade-offs with those of the others (e.g. Silverstein 1997; Rampton 2001; Goodwin 2007).

These qualifications gain weight when we consider current internet phenomena. In the iterative part of internet-based social action, the influence of algorithmic processes needs to be taken seriously. Such algorithmic processes are often described by means of terms such as 'echochamber effects' or 'bubble effects' (Pariser 2011; Tufekci 2015; van Nuenen 2016), and they refer to the fact that machines organizing activity in social media environments, create communities of people who (in the views of those designing such algorithms) should 'share' something – interests, social characteristics, opinions and so forth. Even if there is presently hardly a way in which we can profoundly and directly examine this (these algorithms are among the best-kept industrial secrets) there is little doubt that their effects reinforce and enlarge the iterative features of actions, perhaps pushing them even towards new levels of generic uniformity. Research on this is, as said, extremely difficult, but when investigating online actions, it is wise to keep an awareness that not everything we observe is an effect of deliberate human choice and agency, but an artefact of algorithmic agency.

This genre theory has methodological consequences: the validity of examples in analysis, including complex ones, rests on their generic recognizability, on the fact that through and beyond their unique situatedness we can spot the larger, historical genre templates invoked in such social actions. Every instance of social action is evidently unique, *but only to a degree*. For it is also generic, and in that sense always a token of a type, 'representative' of that type. The genre theory, therefore, can be seen as the grounding for an ethnography that satisfies the demand both for ecological validity and for representativeness.

4.4 A microhegemonic theory of identity

Building on to what has been established so far, I now move on to two theories that are sides of the same coin: a theory of identity, followed by another one of social groups that essentially extends the former. While there is no sensible way in which we can talk of identity without talking about the social groups in which identities are performed and enregistered, I separate them here for clarity's sake, because identity and social groups are, in many studies, isolated as separate domains of study.

Communicative practice is always and invariably an act of identity. Sociolinguists have taken this insight on board since the mid-1980s (Le Page and Tabouret-Keller 1985), turning it, as Allan Bell observes, into one of the most productive topics of sociolinguistic research in recent years (Bell 2016). Very few sociolinguists need to be convinced of the *performative* and *creative* nature of identity (in other words, of identity not as a given but as something that emerges in social action); of its *dialogical* nature (creating a difference between *enacted* and *ascribed* identities), of the *plurality* of identities; of the dynamics of *'serious' and 'ludic'* identity work prevalent in practices such as 'styling'; and of identity as a *problem* central to a complex politics of performance and ascription (for surveys, see De Fina, Schiffrin and Bamberg 2006; Coupland and Jaworski 2009; sophisticated examples include Harris 2006; Rampton 2006; Møller 2017). So here too, we can draw extensively on sociolinguistic insights.

This could be helpful, for the problem of categorization (another word for identity ascription) is an old one in social and humanities research, notably in quantitative ones where a degree of stability in research design is mandatory across the sample (Cicourel 1974). There is an assumption that every subject can (and perhaps should) be determined as to identity by describing him/her along essential bureaucratic parameters such as nationality, age, gender, social class, ethnicity, religious affiliation, profession – extended, sometimes, to include educational qualifications, income, family relationships, sexuality and health status. And this, let us note, is where we continue to feel the full weight of the Durkheimian tradition in research, for those are the diacritics of the modern 'thick' communities that have preoccupied macro-sociological research in the tradition we associate with him. The assumption, reformulated, is that we can know and understand society when we divide it into segments and relationships based on these identity categories.

In contrast to that tradition, I propose to see identities as *chronotopically organized moralized behavioural scripts*; above I suggested the term 'microhegemonies' as shorthand for that contorted phrase. And I will explain what I mean by that.

Let us recapitulate some of the elements in Sabrina Billings's study of the role of language in Tanzanian beauty contests, discussed above. We saw how the use of language – particular forms of English, to be more precise – was a key part of a larger set of features deployed by the contenders and judged by the audience and the jury in relation to perceived norms of 'good' conduct in such events. In fact, what we saw was that 'beauty queen' – an ascribed identity category – needed to be *performed* by enacting a set of different, dispersed 'qualities' – beauty, intelligence, education levels, humour – of which perceived fluency in 'good' English was emblematic. I emphasized that this normative system was polycentric and scaled, with local and nonlocal norms piled up onto one another, and that the judgement passed by the audience when one of the contenders failed to display the expected fluency in 'good' English was a moral judgement of the entire person: she was seen and condemned as a phony.

The judgement, an identity judgement, was a *moralization* of the degree of normativity perceived in the contender's display of a composite set of behavioural norms – a behavioural script that needs to be followed to some degree of satisfaction – which was specific to the occasion of the beauty pageant. It was *chronotopic*.

The latter is of critical importance. We long know from a wide and highly diverse literature that people do not 'have' an identity but perform identities. In the observable conduct of people, there is no such thing as 'identity': we can observe concrete, situated and interactionally contextualized identity work. This contextualization is of paramount importance: we need to adjust our identity work to the highly specific demands of particular contexts. To unpack that last term: 'context', in actual fact, is a concrete time-space configuration in which particular forms of identity are expected, required or optional, and in which, consequently, we need to deploy highly particular resources drawn from what we can conveniently call 'identity repertoires' (cf. Blommaert 2005: 234; Blommaert and De Fina 2017). To put it concretely: the beauty pageant, with its complex layered normative orientations to global and local diacritics of success and failure, is a specific chronotope. The contenders can only be given the identity of 'beauty queen' in the time-space configuration of the pageant; outside of it, a contender would be an office clerk, somebody's daughter, a student, and what not. 'Beauty queen' and the behavioural scripts out of which it is constructed, are things that are specific to that one particular chronotope – just as bicycle racers can only call themselves 'world champion' when they have won one particular race, the world championship race. Identity work, in that sense, is never all over the place, it is very much connected to specific time-space niches.

Chronotopes help us get a precise grip on what we mean (referring back to Section 4.1) by mobility in this stage of online–offline globalization. We perpetually move from one chronotope into another, then back to the first and on to a third, and so forth. And we can describe in detail how such moves actually proceed, in physical as well as in sociocultural, politicized space. A shift from one chronotope into another, we can see, involves a massive shift in identity opportunities and criteria of judgement: what works well in one chronotopic environment may backfire in another, and vice versa. Lian Malai Madsen's (2015) study of a martial arts club in Copenhagen is a case in point. The club is superdiverse in composition and counts a large number of young Copenhagers with a migration background. These youngsters are publicly seen and often described as 'poorly integrated' and marginalized both educationally and in the labour market. They are widely perceived as a social problem. But in the martial arts club, they are often the stars, the centres of attention and bearers of prestige and status as champions. In the club, we see a carnivalesque reversal of everything these youngsters are outside of it. Their skills, competences and patterns of performance – the same ones as those that give them the negative ascribed identities mentioned a moment ago – are valued as fully integrated, as signs of extraordinary capability and even as exemplary models to be emulated by others.

In Madsen's study, we see quite profound identity shifts sequentially, as subjects move from one chronotope into another one. Chronotopes can and do simultaneously overlap as well – this is one of the aspects of what I call polycentricity. A mathematics class, for instance, is of course an institutionally regimented chronotope in which form and contents are tightly scripted and policed by the teacher; but that class may *at the same time* be seen as a congregation of teenage peer groups, an entirely different chronotope following a (sometimes dramatically) different set of normative behavioural expectations than those imposed by the school and the teacher, and displaying a highly different dynamics of identity as well. The underperforming student in the eyes of the teacher may be, because of exactly the *same* behavioural features, the coolest kid in class and a role model in the eyes of his/her peers. In fact, we can see Goffman's (1959) famous distinction between 'front stage' and 'backstage' as two simultaneously overlapping chronotopes, each with their own modes of social action, identity affordances and systems of normative organization; and many of the interaction rituals he described can be reconsidered as microhegemonies specific to particular chronotopic environments as well (Goffman 1967, also 1961, 1981; see also Silverstein 2005). Goffman's oeuvre, in fact, can be seen as a consistent engagement with how Americans in his time organized their social relations through forms of interactional behaviour adjusted to the chronotopes they inhabited – hence titles such as 'Relations in Public' or 'The Lecture'(Goffman 1971, 1981: Chapter 4).

Goffman described the microhegemonies of an offline society. It is evident that the online social space has enabled a multiplication of available chronotopes and relations between chronotopes, and thus generates a wide range of new modes of identity work. Since a tremendous amount of research is presently in the process of being rolled out, I must confine myself here to a general summary of available insights, and start with some comments on the particular communicative *practices* we observe in the online world (for surveys see

Leppänen and Peuronen 2012; Androutsopoulos 2016; Varis and van Nuenen 2017: Leppänen, Westinen and Kytölä 2017).

1 In a general sense, the emergence of online communication as a feature of everyday life has dramatically increased the importance of **literacy**, and more specifically of multimodal literacy. Online communication is overwhelmingly written (or 'designed': Kress 2003; Jewitt 2013). Writing, as we know, is a field of normativity which is structured quite differently from spoken discourse – writing 'errors' are often treated with considerably less tolerance than errors in speech – but, at the same time, online writing practices display an incredible dynamism and innovativeness dislodging the traditional boundaries of 'writing' (and, evidently, those of language in its traditional sense). Consider the now widespread use of emoticons and expressions such as 'OMG' and 'LOL', the influence of AAVE-based hip-hop register in new genres of mobile and online communication (Kytölä and Westinen 2015), the complex blends of visual, textual, static and dynamic features of contemporary websites, and, especially, the phenomenon of 'memes' (Du 2016). People do very different things in and with semiotic material online, compared to what they do in offline contexts.

2 Much of what is done, especially on social media, appears to be what is known as **phatic communion**: the transmission and exchange of messages in which not propositional content ('information') appears to be a central concern, but the maintenance of 'convivial' social relations and the performance of specific acts of identity – that of, for example, a 'friend' by means of Facebook 'likes', a 'follower' by means of Twitter retweets, or just an 'acquaintance' by means of quick and short mobile messages (Miller 2008; Jones 2014; Varis and Blommaert 2013; Velghe 2013).

3 The boundaries between online and offline social processes are **porous**. Registers of online activities such as Mass Online Games can spill over into the everyday vocabulary of gamers and become new indexicals for expressing social ties (Sierra 2016), and online activities become a learning environment where resources are built and circulated that are useful offline and now also profoundly influence such offline practices (Leppänen 2007; Maly and Varis 2015; Blommaert 2016d). Conversely, offline identity features can influence the choice and use of specific online platforms and modes of conduct (boyd 2011). And, of course, new phenomena such as online dating are meant to go offline as soon as the first online steps have been completed (Toma 2016). The internet has also become an enormous repository of explicitly didactic and normative material – the 'how to?' genre – in which people can get clear instructions for how to perform specific forms of identity (Blommaert and Varis 2015).

4 Even so, online forms of self-presentation have **characteristics and affordances of their own,** not reducible to existing offline resources. Given the absence, in general, of face-to-face contact, people can hide behind an alias and construct entirely fictional personae for themselves – something that characterizes the darker side of the online social world (boyd 2014: 100). But in more benign ways, there is a tendency to present oneself in the 'my best day' mode – the way one wishes to be perceived by others (Baron 2008: 71; boyd 2014). There is also a plethora of new and reconfigured discursive genres, ranging from 'Wiki'-like formats of collaborative writing to particular modes of confessional narrative, raising issues of privacy and the limits of self-exposure (cf. Page 2012; van Nuenen 2016). The online world is a space where distinct forms of identity work can be performed, only distantly connected to what goes on elsewhere.

In spite of this final remark, all of the above implies that quite a bit of contemporary identity work is carried over and oscillates between online and offline contexts, creating highly intricate connections between, for instance, what is microhegemonically expected or permitted in the chronotope of Facebook and that of the school playground (think of cyber bullying) or the workplace (think of employers monitoring employees' social media accounts). The chronotopic nature of identities thus now evidently creates an enormous panorama of possible and expected identities, vastly more than those captured by the bureaucratic, 'thick' diacritics I mentioned at the outset. The variation of chronotopes we move through in social life demands, and endows us with, a plethora of 'light' identities, if you wish, not excluding the old and established 'thick' categories but complementing them – 'big' diacritics such as race, gender, class or ethnicity are not absent, but they are performed in different and sometimes surprising ways (e.g. Rampton 2006; Harris 2006; boyd 2011; Goebel 2013, 2015; Wang 2015; Faudree 2015; Fox and Sharma 2016).

At the level of everyday experience, however, our identities and those of others depend strongly on *details* of behaviour and appearance, of which a certain amount needs to be displayed and performed – identities, one can see, are judged on the basis of perceptions of 'enoughness' (Blommaert and Varis 2015; also Goebel 2013). We can see a reflex of the genre theory of social action here: identity work is evidently genre-based, and it will display the same calibration between tendencies towards similarity and tendencies towards deviation as the one we encountered when we discussed genres.

4.5 A theory of 'light' social groups

The discussion of identity already showed that the 'thick' diacritics of identity are not out, but that they are in need of a more delicate balancing with a wide range of other, 'light' forms of identity. To name just two, social class is not out, and neither is ethnicity – but both are now imaginable as far more 'styled' than 'given' identities, drawn from within a repertoire of identities that contains lots of different orientations. This obviously has a bearing on the discussion of social groups as well.

This discussion has a very long pedigree. Classics of sociology address society as their object, and attempt to find and express the rules that guide it. Sociology, it is said, is the science of society. How such a society should be defined, however, has been a consistent bone of contention since the very early days of sociology as a science. Generally speaking, authors reserve the term 'society' for the perceived *permanent* features of a social system, often (as by Durkheim and Parsons) ad hoc circumscribed by the nation-state. Such features were believed to be less subject to rapid or radical change – as distinct from features that were seen as superficial, transient or less reliable as indicators of social structure.

Here is what Georg Simmel had to say about it. Noting that the sociology of his era still had to prove its right to exist, notably against proponents of Methodological Individualism, Simmel emphasizes the fact of interaction as the eminently social phenomenon – see above – and then observes:

> It is only a superficial attachment to linguistic usage (a usage quite adequate for daily practice) which makes us reserve the term 'society' for *permanent* interactions only. More specifically, the interactions we have in mind when we talk about 'society' are crystallized as definable, consistent structures such as the state and the family, the guild and the church, social classes and organizations based on common interests. (1950: 9, italics in original)

We have already encountered the same tendency towards preferring such 'thick' and permanent forms of organization in the work of Parsons, who focused on the governing pattern of values and their integrative effects to characterize society, while smaller and 'lighter' social groups were said to be tied together by norms – with the interactions between both resulting, sometimes, in contradictions and disorder. This hierarchical ranking in which society is presented as organized, primarily, by strong ties within 'thick' communities such as those listed by Simmel (the state, church, etc.) and, secondarily, by 'lighter' ties within a plethora of social groups, of course did not prevent attention to the latter. But studies of smaller social sub-groups often articulated an awareness of their relatively superficial and ephemeral character. See, for instance, how Bourdieu and Passeron describe the Parisian student community of the 1960s:

> The student milieu is possibly less integrated today than ever before. ... Everything leads us, thus, to doubt whether students, effectively, constitute a homogeneous, independent and integrated social group. (1964: 54–5, French original, my translation)

Homogeneity, independence or autonomy, and level of integration, thus, decide the kind of social group formed by students: quite a poor one compared to, for instance, social class. And one should not be carried away by the lure of superficial groupness:

> Students can have common practices, but that should not lead us to conclude that they have identical experiences of such practices, or above all a collective one. (Bourdieu and Passeron 1964: 24–5)

Precisely the same argument was used by Goffman in *Encounters* (1961) when he described poker players as a tightly focused community of people otherwise unacquainted, in which clear and transparent rules of conduct were shared (and assumed to be shared as soon as someone joins a poker game). Goffman saw such brief moments of tight but temporary and ephemeral groupness as aggregations of people sharing just the rules of the encounters, but little beyond it. Such 'light' groups, or 'groupings whose boundaries we know very little about' (Goffman 1971: xxiv), could be studied as a way to arrive at insights into fundamental social procedures such as socialization and identity development (see e.g. Becker et al. 1961 for a classic). But when it comes to understanding society (the real thing), attention should go to the 'thick' communities, and amendments to the established set of 'thick' communities, potentially dislodging the consensus about its consistency and stability, invariably led to considerable controversy.[8]

Simmel, we saw, expressed an awareness of the conventional – untheorized – nature of this consensus about the scope of 'society'. And after mentioning 'the state and the family, the guild and the church, social classes and organizations based on common interests' as the stereotypical arenas for 'permanent interactions', he goes on:

> But in addition to these, there exist an immeasurable number of less conspicuous forms of relationships and kinds of interaction. Taken singly, they may appear negligible. But since in actuality they are inserted into the comprehensive and, as it were, official social formations, they alone produce society as we know it. ... On the basis of the major social formations – the traditional subject matter of social science – it would be similarly impossible to piece together the real life of society as we encounter it in our experience. (Simmel 1950: 9)[9]

In other words – and here is a methodological invective of considerable importance – if we intend to understand 'society as we know it', we need to examine these 'less conspicuous forms of relationships and kinds of interaction' not instead of but alongside 'the major social formations'. We can only get access to the necessarily abstract 'society' by investigating the on-the-ground micropractices performed by its members (called *sociation* by Simmel), taking into account that these micropractices may diverge considerably from what we believe characterizes society and may eventually show complex ties connecting practices and features of social structure (cf. Collins 1981; Goffman 1971: 196).[10]

The problem is familiar for sociolinguists: 'Language' with a capital L can only be examined by investigating its actual situated forms of usage; and while many prefer to define Language as a stable, autonomous and homogeneous object, the actual forms of usage are characterized by bewildering variability, diversity and changeability. I have already explained that, in addition, sociolinguists began to understand quite a while ago that very little can be learned from Language about the actual social functions and effects of language. In other words: understanding what language is and does, in the realities of social life, forces us to take the variable, diverse and dynamic actual forms of language usage ('speech') as our object, even if they cannot immediately be squeezed into a normative framework of Language. Even more: a privileged site for research, offering analytical breakthroughs of momentous importance, is the small and highly heterogeneous peer group where the boundaries of languages, and of the 'major social formations', are blurred (e.g. Gumperz 1982; Rampton 2006; Harris 2006; Jørgensen 2008).

Yet, recall the action theory sketched above: we should start from actions rather than from participants and their characteristics and put *sociation* ahead of society.[11] Sociolinguistics can offer a simple four-step methodological programme for empirical investigations into groups of any kind and configuration. Here it is:

1 Patterns of communication necessarily involve meaningful social relationships as prerequisite, conduit and outcome.

2 Such relationships will always, similarly, involve identities and categorizations, interactionally established.

3 Thus, when observing patterns of communication, we are observing the very essence of sociation and 'groupness' – regardless of how we call the groups.

4 And specific patterns of interaction shape specific forms of groups.

In this sociolinguistic frame, thus, we approach groups pragmatically and axiologically, from the angle of the actual observable communication practices and through the values attributed to such practices. Groups, then, are not collections of human beings but patterned sets of communicative behaviours and the relationships with which they are dialectically related. Whenever we see such ordered forms of communicative behaviour, there is an assumption of active and evolving groupness – sociation – but the analytical issue is not the nature of the group (or the label we need to choose for it) but the specific social relationships observable through and in communication – a Batesonian focus, if you wish, overtaking a Durkheimian one. All other aspects of sociation can be related to this. So if one needs the definition of a group: a group is a communicatively organized and ratified set of social relationships.

We can extend these insights now and bring them into the broader field of social action. The theoretical core of what follows can be summarized in this way:

1 Online social practices generate a broad range of entirely new forms of 'light' communities.

2 In the online–offline social contexts we inhabit, understanding social action requires attention to such 'light' groups alongside 'thick' groups.

3 Because in the everyday lived experience of large numbers of people, membership of 'light' communities prevails over that of 'thick' communities.

4 'Light' communities, thus, display many of the features traditionally ascribed to 'thick' communities.

5 Even more: if we wish to comprehend contemporary forms of social cohesion, we need to be aware of the prominent role of 'light' communities and 'light' practices of conviviality as factors of cohesion.

Let me briefly elaborate the very first point. For those who wonder whether the internet has created anything new in the way of social formations: yes, it has. Social media, in particular, have generated groups never previously attested: tremendously large communities of users, who – contrary to television audiences – *actively* contribute to the contents and interaction patterns of new media. Facebook's 1.79 billion users constitute a media-using community that has no precedent in history; the approximately ten million people who play the mass online game *World of Warcraft* are another type of unprecedented community; and so are the 50 million people who use the Tinder dating app to find a suitable partner.

All of these communities are formed by individuals voluntarily and actively joining them to perform entirely novel forms of social practice. Membership of such groups is experienced by many of its members as indispensable in everyday life, even if the practices performed in such groups would not always be seen as vital or indicative of one's core identity – these are 'light' groups and 'ludic' practices. But in addition to these voluntary communities, the internet generates *involuntary* communities through its algorithmic functions, bringing people together in networks of perceived shared interests and profiles, of which members are often unaware. The internet, thus, generates a range of new *performed* identities as well as a range of new *ascribed* identities; whereas the former usually function as spaces for interpersonal interaction and knowledge exchange among users, the latter's function is opaque for the ascribed members, who are categorized in terms of third-party priorities ranging from marketing to intelligence gathering and security concerns.

Having established this elementary point, I must now turn to the online–offline nexus and review some relevant research on how the interplay of online and offline identity resources enables such specific forms of communities to be formed.

In a recent paper, Ico Maly and Piia Varis (2015) show how the now well-known urban 'hipster' communities must be seen as a typical instance of Appadurai's vernacular globalization. While hipsters have become a globalized phenomenon, their actual occurrence, characteristics and social positions are locally determined, jointly yielding a polynomic and microhegemonic identity field. The global features of the groups are largely internet-based imageries of lifestyle, consumption ethos, outlook and commodity orientation (think of the coffee cult, beards, skinny jeans, iPhones and vintage glasses as emblematic features), and the internet offers, as Maly and Varis demonstrate, an ocean of 'how to' resources for aspiring (or insecure) hipsters around the world. The internet, thus, functions as a learning environment for the various norms that shape and police hipster culture. Included in such norms are fine discursive identity distinctions that refer to the hipster label itself:

> We can thus distinguish social groups that dress like hipsters, share an identity discourse based on authenticity, and frequent hipster places. They distance themselves from another group of people they call hipsters: a 'real' hipster is someone who rejects being part of a social group, and thus also rejects the hipster label which is reserved for people who desperately want to be 'hip' and are thus not 'real' or authentic. Nor are they true innovators or trendsetters, which the individualistic, authentic hipsters are. (Maly and Varis 2015: 10)

Thus, there is a strong tendency to self-identify as a non-mainstream, authentic, countercultural individualist, which, however, goes hand in hand with an exuberant and highly self-conscious neoliberal (and, thus, mainstream) consumerism, scaffolded by a globalized 'tight fit' fashion industry. As an effect, this quest for individualism results in a remarkable, global, degree of uniformity. Hipsters are eminently recognizable as hipsters, even if local accents do count and carry local identity values, and even if the usual fractality of orders of indexicality allows for emerging subdivisions within hipsterdom, such as the 'mipster' (Muslim Hipster).

Maly and Varis propose the term 'translocal micropopulation' to describe hipsters, and it is easy to think of other globalized lifestyle communities for whom this label might be suitable – think of Hip-Hop, Rasta, Metal or Gothic communities, but also of 'fashionistas' and 'foodies', of Premier League soccer fans and so forth. All these micropopulations could be more finely described as groups of people who are translocally connected as what we could call *communities of knowledge*, while locally they occur as *communities of practice*. The latter term is better known, and Lave and Wenger (1991) used it to describe groups whose frequent interaction provides a learning environment for rules and norms – not unlike Goffman's (1961) acquaintances in their encounters or Becker et al.'s (1961) medical school students – and knowledge is evidently, in Lave and Wenger's view, an ingredient of practice.

Theirs was, however, an 'offline' description, and what we see in the context of hipsters and other contemporary globalized lifestyle groups is that the internet has become an infrastructure for *separate* and *specific* forms of knowledge gathering and circulation not constricted by the experiences of face-to-face interaction, and so enabling a far wider scope and depth of scaled and polycentric community formation. We are facing a new type of social formation here: a 'light' community that differs from the 'major social formations' listed by Simmel, transcending the diacritics often thought to be essential in understanding social action, and (returning to Bourdieu and Passeron's criteria of social groupness) displaying a high degree of homogeneity, autonomy, integration and structure over and beyond their diversity. We see, for instance, how such groups can be hierarchically structured, with 'teachers', 'experts' and 'learners' in clearly defined relationships vis-à-vis each other, enacted through specific modes of interaction.

The capacity of the internet for generating such translocal communities of knowledge is immense, and we are only beginning to explore this phenomenon – and to take it seriously as a relevant feature of the sociological imagination. Such communities of knowledge are usually just that: online communities or 'fora' where information on an endless variety of topics is exchanged and debated, often through the hierarchical learning relationships just mentioned (e.g. Kytölä 2013; Hanell and Salö 2015; Mendoza-Denton 2015). But the internet has also enabled the emergence of a new form of translocal political community mobilization, and it is impossible to understand contemporary political and social dynamics without looking into such web-based communities of knowledge (cf. McCaughey and Ayers 2003; Graeber 2009). In fact, some of the most high-profile political events of the past decade were internet phenomena: Wikileaks and its release of hacked classified documents, the Panama Papers revealing shocking amounts of money hidden in offshore tax havens, and the alleged Russian hacking of the Democratic Party computers and its possible effect on the election of Donald Trump as US president in November 2016 (e.g. Brevini, Hintz and McCurdy 2013).[12] And in recent years, communities that started online have won offline electoral victories as bona fide political parties – think of Syriza in Greece and Podemos in Spain.

Such processes of online community formation also occur where one would least expect it, and some of the most impressive findings come from China, a country known to maintain a restrictive internet censorship policy. Caixia Du's (2016) study of the online activities of the Chinese precariat can serve to illustrate this. Due to China's economic surge, millions of young and highly educated people have become employed in precarious administrative and technical jobs. These people, Du argues, share acute feelings of disenfranchisement: low income and insecure jobs have placed them in the margins of a society increasingly focused on material success and conspicuous consumption. Since they are digitally literate and since there are hardly any spaces for unimpeded sociopolitical dissidence in China, these people articulate and share their experiences online. Du describes how this large community – a 'class in the making' as she calls it – develops its own secret language through the clever manipulation of memes, sufficiently sophisticated to mislead the censor's search engines. The community also constructs and shares an emblematic culture called *e'gao* and revolving around parody and persiflage of prestigious cultural objects; and its members have created a distinct identity label for themselves: *diaosi*, a derogatory term signifying 'losers' (see also Li, Spotti and Kroon 2014; Yang, Tang and Wang 2015). These 'soft', cultural practices, Du insists, show the gradual coming into being of a previously non-existent social formation in China: a large precariat, critical of the government and billionaire elites and a potential source of large-scale social unrest in China. And all of this happens online.

'Light' communities, we can see, appear to have 'thick' characteristics and modes of practice. There are reasons to believe, consequently that the 'light' practices that characterize so much of the online interactions – think of liking, endorsing, sharing, retweeting on social media – are not as light as one might think. Their main functions, one suggests, are the establishment and maintenance of relationships of conviviality (Varis and Blommaert 2013). But we should not forget that conviviality is an elementary and crucial form of social conduct within established communities – very much like greeting neighbours or exchanging Christmas wishes with friends and relatives. They could as well be seen as 'light' practices with a 'thick' effect: social cohesion within online groups and, increasingly, also spilling over into the offline world.

4.6 A polycentric theory of social integration

Integration continues to be used as a keyword to describe the processes by means of which 'outsiders' – immigrants, usually – need to 'become part' of their 'host culture'. I have put quotation marks around three crucial terms here, and the reasons why will become clear shortly. Integration in this specific sense, of course, has been a central sociological concept in the Durkheim–Parsons tradition. A society is a conglomerate of social groups held together by integration: the sharing of (a single set of) central values which define the character, the identity (singular) of that particular society (singular). And it is this specific sense of the term that motivates complaints – a long tradition of them – in which immigrants are blamed for not being 'fully integrated', or more specifically, 'remaining stuck in their own culture' and 'refusing' to integrate in their host society.

Half a century ago, in a trenchant critique of Parsons, C. Wright Mills (1959: 47) observed that historical changes in societies must inevitably involve shifts in the modes of integration. Several scholars documented such fundamental shifts – think of Bauman, Castells, Beck and Lash – but mainstream discourses, academic and lay, still continue to rely on the monolithic and static Parsonian imagination. In what follows I shall draw on the action-centred perspective developed above and propose that new modes of diaspora, now conditioned by access to new forms of mediated communication enabling new modes of interaction, do indeed result in new modes of integration.

To formulate this as a theoretical proposition: *people are integrated in a wide variety of communities, both 'thick' and 'light' ones, and to differing degrees.* A 'completely integrated' individual is an individual who has achieved such diverse forms of integration and is able to move from one community to another while shifting between the modes of integration expected in each of them.

Let us look at some corroborating research. In a splendid dissertation, Jelke Brandehof (2014; for a similar study, see Nemcova 2016; also Tall 2004) investigated the ways in which a group of Cameroonian doctoral students at Ghent University (Belgium) used communication technologies in their interactions with others. She investigated the technologies proper – mobile phone and online applications – as well as the language resources used in specific patterns of communication with specific people. Figure 4.1 is a graphic representation of the results for one male respondent (Brandehof 2014: 38).

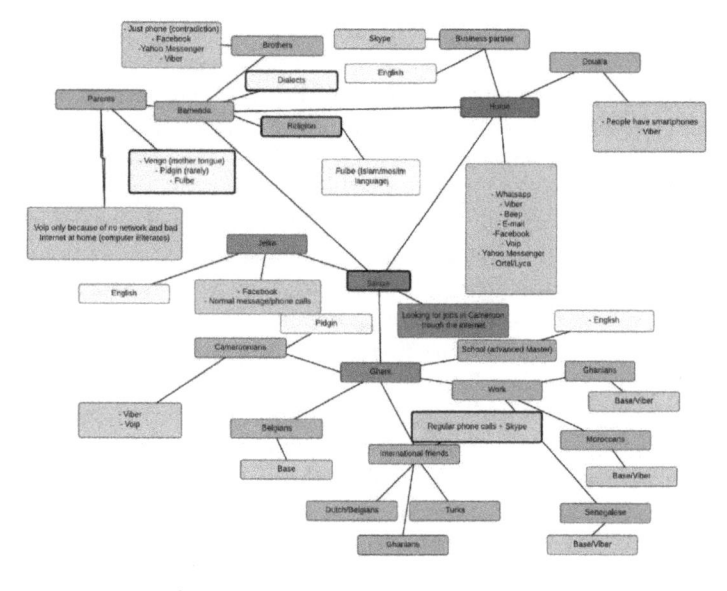

FIGURE 4.1 *The communication network of a Cameroonian student in Ghent. Courtesy: Jelke Brandehof.*

This figure, I would argue, represents the empirical side of integration – *real* forms of integration in contemporary diaspora situations. Let me elaborate this.

The figure, no doubt, looks extraordinarily complex; yet there is a tremendous amount of order and nonrandomness to it. We see that the Cameroonian man deploys a wide range of technologies and platforms for communication: his mobile phone provider (with heavily discounted rates for overseas calls) for calls and text messages, Skype, Facebook, Beep, Yahoo Messenger, different VoIP systems, WhatsApp and so forth. He also uses several different languages: standard English, Cameroonian pidgin, local languages (called 'dialects' in the figure) and Fulbe (other respondents also reported Dutch as one of their languages). And he maintains contacts in three different sites: his own physical, economic and social environment in Ghent, his home environment in Cameroon, and the virtual environment of the labour market in Cameroon. In terms of activities, he maintains contacts revolving around his studies, maintaining social and professional networks in Ghent, job-hunting on the internet and an intricate range of family and business activities back in Cameroon. Each of these activities – here is the order and nonrandomness – involves a conscious choice of medium, language variety and addressee. Interaction with his brother in Cameroon is done through smartphone applications and in a local language, while interactions with other people in the same location, on religious topics, are done in Fulbe, a language marked as a medium among Muslims.

As mentioned earlier, specific forms of interaction assume specific forms of sharedness and shape specific forms of groups. Our subject is integrated, through the organized use of these communication resources, in several groups situated in very different zones of social life. He is integrated in his professional and social environment in Ghent, in the local casual labour market where students can earn a bit on the side, in the Cameroonian labour market where his future lies, and in his home community. Note that I use a *positive* term here: he is integrated in all of these zones that make up his life, because his life develops in real synchronized time in these different zones, and all of these zones play a vital part in this subject's life. He remains integrated as a family member, a friend, a Muslim and a business partner in Cameroon, while he also remains integrated in his more directly tangible environment in Ghent – socially, professionally and economically. Note, of course, that some of these zones coincide with the 'thick' groups of classical sociology (the nation-state, family, religion) while others can better be described as 'light' communities – the student community, the workplace, web-based networks and so forth.

This level of simultaneous integration across groups, both 'thick' and 'light' ones, is *necessary*. Our subject intends to complete his doctoral degree work in Ghent and return as a highly qualified knowledge worker to Cameroon. Rupturing the Cameroonian networks might jeopardize his chances of reinsertion in a lucrative labour market (and business ventures) upon his return there. While he is in Ghent, part of his life is spent there while another part continues to be spent in Cameroon, for very good reasons. The simultaneity of integration in a variety of zones, however, should not lead us to suggest that the *degrees* of integration would be similar. We can assume that our subject is more profoundly integrated in, for instance, his family and religious communities in Cameroon, than in the Ghent-based casual labor market, where he needs to rely on the advice and support of others to find his way around.

I emphasized that our subject has to remain integrated across these different zones – *sufficiently* integrated, not 'completely' integrated. And the technologies for cheap and intensive long-distance communication enable him to do so. This might be the fundamental shift in 'modes of integration' we see since the turn of the century: diaspora no longer entails a total rupture with the places and communities of origin; neither, logically, does it entail a 'complete integration' in the host community, because there are instruments that enable one to lead a far more gratifying life, parts of which are spent in the host society while other parts are spent elsewhere. In short, here is a textbook example of Castells's 'network society' (1996). We see that diasporic subjects keep one foot in the 'thick' community of family, neighbourhood and local friends, while they keep another foot – on more instrumental terms – in the host society and yet another one in 'light' communities such as internet-based groups and the casual labour market. Together, they make up a late-modern diasporic life.

There is nothing exceptional or surprising to this: the jet-setting European professional business class members do precisely the same when they go on business trips: smartphones and the internet enable them to make calls home and to chat with their daughters before bedtime, and to inform their social network of their whereabouts by means of social media updates. In that sense, the distance between Bauman's famous 'traveller and vagabond' is narrowing: various types of migrants are presently using technologies previously reserved for elite travellers. And just as the affordances of these technologies are seen as an improvement of a nomadic lifestyle by elite travellers, it is seen as a positive thing by these other migrants, facilitating a more rewarding and harmonious lifestyle that does not involve painful ruptures of existing social bonds, social roles, activity patterns and identities.

What looks like a *problem* from within a Parsonian theory of 'complete integration', therefore, is in actual fact a *solution* for the people performing the 'problematic' behaviour. The problem is theoretical, and rests upon the kind of monolithic and static sociological imagination criticized by C. Wright Mills and others, and upon the distance between this theory and the empirical facts of contemporary diasporic life. Demands for 'complete integration' (and complaints about the failure to do so) can best be seen as nostalgic and, when uttered in political debates, as ideological false consciousness – or more bluntly, as sociological surrealism.

4.7 Constructures

In social science, social structure is very often used as a target of analysis – one intends to say something about the 'structural' level of social organization. And it is also often used as a methodological tool – one identifies a level of social reality called 'structure', and such structures contribute to the analysis of the case examined. Some of the most epochal and influential social-scientific work was work addressing just that: the emergence and solidification of structural dimensions of society – think of the work of Parsons (1937) or that of Giddens (1984). Structure, it seems, is the most 'macro' dimension of social life, and 'structural' is the most general level of statements made in its analysis. In Fernand Braudel's famous distinctions between time-scales, the structural was situated in the realm of the *longue durée*: the time of civilizations, of modes of production, of the climate and the demography of parts of the world (e.g. 1969, 1981). And for C. Wright Mills and several others – think of Weber and Parsons – social structure could be described mainly by attention to the institutional orders within the nation-state, and 'if we understand how these institutional orders are related to one another, we understand the social structure of a society' (Mills 1959: 134). The consensus appears to be that structure refers to phenomena at the level of 'the total society' (Mills 1959: 137) and shows a persistent, slowly developing character. In that sense, work such as that of Appadurai (1996) and Castells (1996) addresses newly emerging structures. By the same token, of course, teleological models of social evolution, such as those of Hegel and Marx, would be structural.

One will have some difficulty finding detailed descriptions of what 'structure' actually *is*, how it can be empirically identified and how it relates to the chaotic specifics of the everyday social processes we can observe. Attempts such as those of Giddens – who was explicit in his definitions of structure – remain open to critique and controversy (see e.g. Thompson 1984: Chapter 4). Mostly, 'structure' is used in a loosely defined way in the sense I outlined above. And once more, if we use what we know about language in social life as the fundamental imagery for social science, we may offer a somewhat more precise set of formulations.

Let me first sketch the field of arguments in which I shall situate my proposals. I wish to keep my distance from two quite widespread frames of reference for discussing structure.

1 First, I want to avoid a particular tradition of interpretation of 'structure'. 'Structure', certainly in a Lévi–Straussian variety of structura*lism*, has acquired strong suggestions of absoluteness, abstractness, predictability, anonymity, a-temporality and staticity. Structure, as the guiding value system of a society, is that which provides enduring stability to a social system and makes it resilient – as Parsons suggested – to the onslaught of cultural revolutions from within youth culture (Parsons 1964). And even if structure is the outcome of active *structuration* at a variety of scale levels in social life (Giddens 1984; Thompson 1984), most scholars would still use the term to describe dominant (if not determining) rules, values or principles driving the development of societies across time-space. It is also quite often presented as a social force operating below the level of consciousness and agency of people, a set of tacit and not always 'emicly' well-understood aspects of social life – as in the 'deep structure' of Chomskyan transformational grammar.

2   Two, I want to avoid a particular set of discursive associations. 'Structure' is often seen as something antagonistic to 'postmodernist' and 'mobility/complexity' approaches to social life. While traditional ('modernist') social science would be on the side of anonymous static structure, 'postmodernist' science would favour individual agency and instability, and thus would become at once 'poststructuralist' – in an unrealistic either/or frame in which methodological preferences appear to lead directly to ontological strictures.[13] It is rarely observed that 'poststructuralist' scholars such as Bourdieu and Foucault did not just reject *any* concept of structure but rejected a specific one: the Lévi–Straussian concept referred to above. They rejected a certain kind of structuralism (and their 'poststructuralism' would be more accurately defined as 'post-Lévi-Straussism') but not 'the structural' as a dimension of social systems.

In general, this false antagonism often renders more nuanced and precise understandings of structure invisible. Many fail to recognize that complexity is not the absence of order, but a different kind of order. I shall therefore use another term to make my point. Rather than using 'structure', I shall use *constructure* in what follows. New terms enable us to examine the validity of the older ones, and they also afford some measure of detachment from unwarranted intertextual readings. 'Constructure' is not technically speaking a neologism – it is an archaic term that offers a felicitous collocation of 'structure' and 'construction'. The latter term, as can be seen, can easily be changed into 'agency', and so we have a concept in which both dimensions, often seen as antagonistic, are heuristically and analytically joined, and in which the layered historicity of social processes can be captured.

The baseline assumption – which, I hope, is entirely uncontroversial – is that any social event is *structured*: there is always 'order' in any observed social event. But from a complexity perspective on sociolinguistic phenomena and processes, this order is always:

1 **Dynamic and unstable:** order is always a temporally contingent quality because systems are perpetually unfolding and changing (e.g. describing language at one point in time will necessarily result in a description which is different from what was current a generation ago as well as from what will be current in the next generation).

2 **Unfinished and stochastic:** given the perpetual change, any momentary observation of order will contain open-ended, quickly evolving features anticipating new forms of order; it will also contain features that are contested and conflictual, and features in the process of being eliminated or established (e.g. archaisms and neologisms, short-lived as well as more lasting ones, are always part of any synchronic observation of language). It is stochastic in the sense that today's structure might be yesterday's exception, and that outcomes are quite often not predictable from initial conditions but 'accidental' or deviant in terms of what was seen as dominant.

3 Non-unified: any form of order consists of a mixture
of different forces, developing at different speeds
and with different scope and range (e.g. the different
registers in anyone's repertoire have different speeds of
development, with 'standard' registers usually slower in
development than, for example, youth registers – hence
our sense of 'trendiness').

As just noted, we are used to reserve the term 'structure'
for the slower, more persistent forces, the *durée*, the macro
dimension of social processes. I suggest we avoid this micro–
macro distinction and consider *the entire mix* when we use
the term 'constructure'. Given the complexity perspective,
there is no telling *a priori* which of the features in the mix
will determine future developments – change often happens in
the margins and begins as a statistical minority or exception,
often negatively qualified or overlooked. Think of the
spectacular rise of emoticons as part of several mainstream
genres of writing nowadays. Emoticons have not replaced
the conventional forms of alphabetic writing – we still write
(roman-alphabetically, at least) from left to right, and we still
use the conventional orthographic symbols we associate with
the written form of the language we are using. Emoticons have
been added to the mix of contemporary writing, so to speak;
they represent what we could call a 'light' feature, blended
with the 'thick' features of conventional orthography. In terms
of functions, too, we should not associate 'structure' *a priori*
with 'thick' functions but do justice to 'light' functions such
as that of conviviality, discussed above. They are, as we saw,
only light from the kind of transcendental structuralism I
dismissed earlier.

Constructures are, thus, a permanently unfolding mix
of various separate structures, the momentary deployment
of which in social practice grants the latter a degree of
orderliness, recognizable and ratifiable for others. Going
back to our theory of social action, we can see how in

constructures, we can unify traditional notions of structure and agency. Rephrased, we have a tool for recognizing the two essential characteristics of social action – iterativity and creativity. Recall, most of the behaviour we deploy socially is overwhelmingly iterative, but slightly inflected by unique, creative and situated performativity. Observe, however, that I do not equate iterativity with stability and creative performativity with change. *The entire mix* is continuously changing, including the 'iterative' aspects of it. Detaching the performative 'accent' from the iterative 'structure' obscures the fact that, for people in everyday practice, the 'accent' is often the essence of what they perceive as meaningful in social action. And it is by means of the performative 'accent' that the iterative features of behaviour are also transformed into unique and creative characteristics of *specific* social actions performed by *specific* people. All of this was made clear earlier when we discussed the genre theory of social action; its relevance here is evident.

Rather than as a concept that points towards the stability of social systems – the simplistic interpretation of structure, noted above – constructure thus points to the permanently changing nature of social systems *and* to the way they change. This might explain why parts of past reality remain recognizable while other parts are not. When we read Erving Goffman's observations on social life in the United States of the 1950s and 1960s, for instance, we can still recognize a great deal of it today, even if much of our social life these days is performed in a social space that did not exist in Goffman's world: the virtual space of social media. Interaction in this virtual world is organized along different sets of norms many of which differ strongly from the ones Goffman detected in face-to-face engagements. Online sociality, however, has not *replaced* the Goffmanian world of social interaction – the mix has changed, which is why we can still recognize ourselves in Goffman's work, even if we realize that large chunks of our lives are led in very different ways. The constructures have changed.

4.8 Anachronism as power

Finally, I also propose a theory of power; not a general theory of power per se but a *specific* one, about one kind of institutional power. Two points of departure underlie the effort here.

1 In *The Utopia of Rules*, David Graeber describes the fundamental stupidity of contemporary bureaucratization, observing the spread of what he calls 'power without knowledge', 'where coercion and paperwork largely substituted for the need for understanding … subjects' (2015: 65). The contemporary power of bureaucrats often involves an assumption of total knowledge (articulated, e.g. in Foucault's work). Graeber, however, disagrees: 'Situations of structural violence invariably produce extremely lopsided structures of imaginative identification' (69). Rulers have no clue about who and what their subjects are, what it is they do, what they attach importance to, how they live. The schematization and simplification of bureaucracy serve as a substitute for intimate and experience-based knowledge but evidently fail to match up to that.

2 A decent amount of applied-linguistic work, notably on bureaucratic procedures such as asylum applications, shows how transnational subjects, often carrying the traces of a chequered diasporic biography, are caught in entirely unrealistic administrative templates in which their 'origins' are determined on the basis of imaginations of nation-state regimes of bureaucratic identity and on 'modernist' theories of language (cf. Maryns 2006; Blommaert 2001, 2009; Jacquemet 2015). To put it concretely: if applicants' claims as to origin (being from country X) are being disputed, knowledge of the official, national languages of Country X is used as a definitive test. If one fails this criterion, asylum is being denied. The same happens

> whenever an applicant provides discourse which is
> sensed to violate the rules of denotational purity:
> whenever he or she produces contradictions, silences, a
> muddled chronology or a lack (or overload) of detail,
> the applicant is judged to be untrustworthy and the
> success of his or her application is jeopardized.

The 'lopsided structures of imaginative identification' described by Graeber, we can see, in actual fact assume the shape of *anachronisms*: schemes of social imagination, and thus of patterns of meaning-making, perhaps valid in an earlier stage of development, but not adjusted to recent changes and thus inadequate to do justice to the phenomenology of present cases. At the same time, these obsolete schemata are strongly believed to have an unshakeable, persistent relevance as a rationality of administrative information-organization, and are enforced from within that rationality. Thus, an important part of contemporary institutional power is based on anachronisms.

Anachronisms are, of course, an inevitable feature of social change, and we know that governmentality – the logic of institutional bureaucracy and governance – is widely characterized by inertia. It represents a segment of society which develops more slowly than the segments it is supposed to deal with. The gap between the phenomena to be addressed and the schemata by means they are addressed are a grey zone of uncertain understanding and often arbitrary judgement – and thus, increasingly, of miscarriage of justice and of contestation. In terms of research, such anachronistic gaps offer a very rich site for investigating social change itself, based on the general image of 'constructural' social change described above: an image of different layers developing at different speeds. The different speeds manifest themselves in actual, situated cases of misunderstanding (or rather: the *incapacity* for understanding) and/ or of experienced injustice.

The awareness of anachronisms is nothing new, needless to say. Durkheim's own efforts, we have seen, were grounded in his conviction that society had not been adjusted to an important range of innovations caused by the industrialization and urbanization of France. Similar views of an old social order being crushed under the weight of a new one are widespread in the sociological literature. What this theory of anachronisms as power now offers, is *accuracy*. When earlier generations saw their societies being ill adapted to innovation, they could not possibly mean all of society, for the parts that had been innovated were also very much part of that society. What we can contribute, therefore, is a highly precise focus when we look at such phenomena. The anachronisms are *particular modes of organizing social interaction through specific patterns of meaning-making*: categorization, the connection of different phenomena, objects or persons in specific sets of relationships to each other (as when an asylum seeker is brought in a certain relationship with national languages in determining his or her origins), patterns of argumentation and the ways in which we attribute judgements of persuasiveness to certain such patterns. My proposed theory enables us to look for very precise objects of analysis that can document change and the anachronistic effects that accompany it.

Evidently, the internet as an infrastructure for substantial innovation in the modes of social interaction, is prone to such anachronisms. It is a segment of contemporary social life that develops at very high speed, while our modes of meaning-making are slow to be synchronized. Thus, we talk about, and in, new modes of internet communication very much in ways reflecting a pre-internet complex of social relationships. A very clear and simple example of this is the fact that Facebook, the largest social media platform in the world founded in 2004, uses one of the oldest and most primitive terms in the vocabulary for human relationships as its core tool: 'friends'. Evidently, Facebook 'friends' are not necessarily coterminous with offline friends. Facebook also uses a similarly ancient and primitive term to describe the most common interaction function on its platform: 'like'. And evidently, this 'like' function covers a very broad and extraordinarily heterogeneous range of actual meanings. No one needs to actually like an update in order to 'like' it, and no one needs to be an actual friend in order to become a Facebook 'friend' (which is why one can be easily and swiftly 'defriended' whenever differences of opinion arise).

Those are of course innocuous phenomena, merely indexing the anachronistic gaps caused by developments in social media. Less innocent, but very difficult to pinpoint, are the effects of some of the organizing principles behind social media: the algorithmic engines used by, for example, Google and Facebook to bring people, messages and zones of social activity together on the basis of aggregations of huge amounts of ('big') data and metadata generated by users. These algorithms, as mentioned earlier, cannot be directly examined. But some of their effects are known. All of us, I am sure, have at times error-clicked some advertisement on a social media page – say, an advertisement for the newest model of urban SUV by Peugeot. All of us must have noticed how in the days following that erroneous click, multiple automobile advertisements appear on almost any page we open, usually cars in the same price range as the Peugeot we error-clicked. Less visible, perhaps, is the fact that in our social media newsfeeds, we are likely to encounter more people who recently clicked such advertisements in the days following our error-click, most likely people from our contacts network and people in the same geographical area as us. And also less visible, perhaps, is the fact that our perceived interest in cars of a certain brand and price range will be correlated with other data we produce through our social media usage – other products we express an interest in, other aspects of lifestyle, other persons, perhaps political views or preferences for certain sports or sports teams – all of this resulting in a permanently updated 'algorithmic identity', of certain interest for marketing and security professionals, over which we ourselves do not have any control, let alone agency.[14]

Although we can, as I said, gauge these procedures from a distance only, we can infer from what we know that these algorithms are anachronisms too. They are overwhelmingly linear and reductionist: linear, for clicking an item is interpreted as necessarily *rational* and *deliberate* – the mind-reading procedures of the algorithm (manifestly Rational Choice-based) exclude the possibility that we clicked the button by accident, and reductionist, in the sense that clicks are seen as inspired by very specific forms of interest in the thing we clicked – an interest, for instance in buying that object rather than just admiring it or confirming our opinion that such things are absurdly expensive. The algorithmic identities thus ascribed to us may be light years removed from the actual motives driving our social conduct and from the ways in which we see ourselves. Well known, for instance, is that at a certain time when terrorism alert worldwide was red-hot, googling for information on pressure cookers was algorithmically flagged as suspicious because these mundane receptacles happened to be widely used in manufacturing home-made explosive devices. Which is an activity performed, fortunately, by very few individuals. But in order to locate these individuals, a great many more must have come under close scrutiny by security and intelligence officials – for no reason other than, perhaps, they contemplated buying a very nice pressure cooker so as to boost the quality of their bowl of evening soup.

Patterns of human interaction and meaning-making are the most sensitive indicators of social change; every neologism in our everyday language usage demonstrates this. If we wish to understand the fine grain of social change, close attention to these patterns is therefore sure to offer far more analytical purchase than almost any other aspect of social life. Power, too, can be investigated by looking at the anachronisms characterizing patterns of interaction and meaning-making deployed in governance; it can be looked at in very great detail.

Notes

1 One can invoke the authority of Arjun Appadurai here: 'This theory of a break – or rupture – with its strong emphasis on electronic mediation and mass migration, is necessarily a theory of the recent past (or the extended present) because it is only

in the past two decades or so that media and migration have become so massively globalized, that is to say, active across large and irregular transnational terrains' (1996: 9).

2 I reiterate here an assumption already voiced by Anthony Giddens (1976: 127): 'Language as a practical activity is so central to social life that in *some* basic respects it can be treated as exemplifying social processes in general' (italics in original). This assumption, in Giddens's work, does not lead to a structured attention to this 'practical activity', though. See the discussion in J.B. Thompson (1984: Chapter 4).

3 It can therefore also be read as the core of 'superdiversity' as a research programme. See Arnaut (2016); Arnaut, Karrebæk and Spotti (2017); Blommaert and Rampton (2016).

4 Odile Heynders (2016), in an insightful study, examines how such diasporic public spheres have altered the nature and impact of writers as public intellectuals. A variety of 'traditional' social roles is affected by this transformation of the public sphere in which global rock star status is no longer the privilege of sports and entertainment professionals (including US presidents), but now includes the likes of Thomas Piketty, author of a not-too-easily-readable book. Piketty is not the first scientist reaching global celebrity status in spite of the fact that very few of his admirers are able to say what exactly he is arguing for in his work – think of Einstein a century ago – but his fame remains a very rare phenomenon, certainly in a culture in which argumentative complexity is increasingly dispreferred.

5 It is very much worth underscoring this, because of the exceedingly abstract (and unrealistic) ways in which norms and values are being discussed in much academic work and most public debate. Durkheim's own perspective, to his credit, was radically empirical and opposed to *a priori* generalization (Durkheim 1961: 26).

6 One can profitably compare the view articulated here with Agha's (2007b) concept of 'stereotypes' (or 'models', Gal 2016) – indexical complexes to which we orient whenever we communicate and that provide the referenced 'type' of identity of which we provide 'tokens' in our actual communicative conduct. One will find amidst overwhelming agreement two small differences. I emphasize the scaled multiplicity of such 'stereotypes' – the polynomic nature of social conduct – and

suggest a far broader behavioural field of ratification and uptake to be in play. In that sense, I am more inclined towards symbolic interactionism than Agha would, I presume, allow.

7 Read, for instance, Goffman's famous discussion of 'tie-signs' (signs that provide information on the social ties between people, such as e.g. holding hands). Goffman explains that while tie-signs are a culturally encoded resource for identity and social relationship checking, the work of such checking is fraught with complications: 'In Western society tie-signs tend to be inherently ambiguous in the sense that signs can designate relationships of different name, different terms, and different stage – or can entirely and intentionally mislead' (Goffman 1971: 196).

8 One can think of the many energetic debates throughout the twentieth century on the concept and validity of social class as a key sociological notion. Attempts towards 'inventing' new or additional social classes were consistently met with hostility – see, for examples, C. Wright Mills's (1951) description of an emerging 'White Collar' class, and Guy Standing's (2011) proposal for seeing the 'precariat' as a class-on-the-way-in.

9 With this quote Erving Goffman opened his PhD dissertation, and much of Goffman's work can thus be seen as engaging with the baseline 'sociation' processes Simmel outlined, developing within 'less conspicuous forms of relationship and kinds of interaction'. I am grateful to Rob Moore for pointing this out to me.

10 We see affinities here between Simmel's methodological view and phenomenology, especially Husserl's discussion of the 'life-world' as the subjective basis for objectivity (Backhaus 2003).

11 I echo here the critique of Goodwin and Goodwin (2004) against Goffman's (1981) famous distinctions between participants, that left their basic preconceived interactional roles intact (with ratified vs. unratified participants, for instance, still remaining preconceived as 'hearers'). The Goodwins suggested focusing on the actual activities performed by participants in interactions, allowing for a much more fine-grained set of distinctions a posteriori.

12 Trump's own media strategy is sure to become a topic of research in future years as well. Trump systematically rejected what he called 'mainstream mass media', claiming they were

biased, and waged an intensive social media campaign – leading to frequent allegations of 'fake news'. See Maly (2016) for a first appraisal.

13 Nik Coupland walks into the trap of such false antagonism: 'We may have reached a metatheoretical peak in the fetishising of mobility and the antagonistic critiquing of structure, stability, and stasis' (2016: 440 and discussion 440–2).

14 The link between these issues and security concerns cannot be explored fully here, but has been extensively documented and discussed in, for example, Rampton 2016b; Charalambous et al. 2016; Khan 2017.

CHAPTER FIVE

The sociological re-imagination

The world that was puzzling Durkheim has changed and has become the world puzzling Castells and Appadurai. It has changed constructurally: parts of that old world persist while entirely new parts have entered it, most prominently a new global infrastructure for sociality – the internet – which affects the entire planet, including those segments of it where it is rare or absent. The interplay of these different parts demands a new sociological imagination, and my effort towards that goal was guided by a simple assumption: that a number of insights into contemporary patterns of social interaction can be generalized and provide a sociolinguistically animated re-imagination of the social world, characterized by what Arjun Appadurai called vernacular globalization.

Recall what Appadurai meant by this delicate concept: the fact that globalized societies (and there are none that are not globalized) must be comprehended through the interplay of large and small structures, through disciplined attention to the big translocal things and their interactions with the small local ones – what Arnaut, Karrebæk and Spotti (2017) aptly call the 'poeisis-infrastructures nexus'. This nexus is the intersection of locally contextualized practices of meaning-making with higher-scale conditions for meaning-making. The very object of sociolinguistics, in other words. And what sociolinguistics contributes to social science is precisely that: a meticulously empirical perspective on this nexus, in which the object is *the nexus itself* and not its – artificially and counterproductively established – 'micro' and 'macro' dimensions. No contemporary sociolinguist can afford to examine the facts of language in society without considering simultaneously and as part of the same phenomenon, the 'micro' facts of situated discourse and their 'macro'-sociolinguistic conditions of becoming and deployment (cf. Blommaert 2005, 2010). This nexus–object enables us now to propose an empirically grounded (and thus non-speculative and non-'metaphysical') sociological re-imagination – an imagery in which 'the framework of modern society is sought, and within that framework the psychologies of a variety of men and women are formulated', to repeat C. Wright Mills's famous words.

Sociolinguistics does, however, more than that. Theories derived from its evidence cannot subscribe to Methodological Individualism (let alone Rational Choice), as I hope to have established in Chapter 3. They are inevitably grounded in that essential and irreducible social dimension of human life: interaction between people in a comprehensible, and therefore shared, meaningful code following a set of grammars as I called it earlier. All the theories I have proposed here, therefore, contradict and invalidate individualistic views of human behaviour, including so-called neoliberal (or 'postmodern') views of unconstrained social action and unrestricted agency. If action is interaction, it is only partially open to choice, and it is entirely controlled and constrained by the resources available and accessible to the interlocutors *and* to normative-evaluative uptake by others. Our freedom as social agents, to paraphrase this in a different jargon, is seriously curtailed (and *has* to be) as soon as we try to communicate it to others. It remains perplexing to see that a part of social theory has not come to terms with this elementary – defining – fact of communication.

There will be those who ask 'where is power in your theories?' The answer is: everywhere. Sociolinguistic evidence, in my view, compels us to embrace Foucault's conception of power as dispersed, norm-focused and capillary, present in every aspect of social behaviour, and crystallized – often in the form of anachronisms (see section 4.8 above) – in contemporary modes of institutional governmentality. The latter produce and reproduce, let us note, significant amounts of infrastructural violence (Rodgers and O'Neill 2012), by policing access to the normative resources that (often tacitly, as in the case of standard forms of language and literacy: Hymes 1996) condition the realization of what Bourdieu (1982) called 'legitimate language'. The same goes for those resources that control, as do the algorithms and 'big data' directing social media traffic, the shaping of communities and the ascribed identities of their members. The indexical-polynomic organization of normativity in communication makes power *total* and *inevitable* across the entire spectre of observation. I believe we need such a view to start addressing – not a minute too soon – the new forms of power, inequality and conflict that now characterize the online–offline world and of which people such as Edward Snowden, Julian Assange and Chelsea Manning, but also Donald Trump, are uncomfortable reminders.

The same answer will be given to those asking 'where are gender, race, class, ethnicity in your approach?' There, too, we must see that such diacritics are *always* present, but rarely *alone*, usually as part of a polynomic and polycentric pattern of social action in which they co-occur with several other identity resources. As I repeatedly underscored, the 'big' sociological category diacritics are not absent (certainly not when we consider institutional governmentality) but they are as a default *chronotopically niched* and most often *complemented* by a very broad range of other identity 'accents'. Whenever specific identity diacritics are isolated in interaction, they are part of a pattern of generic argumentation that demands careful analysis. I have therefore not hocus-pocussed these big diacritics away, obfuscating racism, sexism and other forms of social category abuse. I have given them, I believe, a very precise location in social action enabling extremely accurate analysis, which should protect us from loose generalization or over-interpretation. For as Dell Hymes rightly proclaimed: 'It is no service to an ethnic group to right the wrong of past exclusion by associating it with shoddy work' (1996: 80).

At the end of the road, the theories I have proposed all revolve around one thing: enabling an accurate description of people's place in society – of who they are, what they are capable of doing, what they effectively do, and what their actions produce in the way of social effect. I consider this a matter of social justice: a science that neglects, marginalizes or dismisses as irrelevant important parts of what people are and do, is a science doomed to generate a deeply flawed image of society. And a governance based on such science is bound to discriminate, incriminate and exclude, which explains my rejection of Rational Choice and related theories as fundamentally flawed instances of sociological imagination, contradicted by all available sociolinguistic evidence. The sociological imagination, we should keep in mind, is a tremendously important and extraordinarily potent political tool; theoretical critique and theoretical reconstruction, therefore, are exercises of substantial 'applied' relevance.

REFERENCES

Adamae, Sonja (2003), *Rationalizing Capitalist Democracy: The Cold War Origins of Rational Choice Liberalism*, Chicago: University of Chicago Press.

Agha, Asif (2003), 'The Social Life of Cultural Value', *Language and Communication*, 23: 231–73.

Agha, Asif (2005), ' Voice, Footing, Enregisterment', *Journal of Linguistic Anthropology*, 15 (1): 38–59.

Agha, Asif (2007a), 'The Object of "Language" and the Subject of Linguistics', *Journal of English Linguistics*, 35: 217–35.

Agha, Asif (2007b), *Language and Social Relations*, Cambridge: Cambridge University Press.

Androutsopoulos, Jannis (2016), 'Theorizing Media, Mediation and Mediatization', in Nikolas Coupland (ed.), *Sociolinguistics: Theoretical Debates*, 282–302, Cambridge: Cambridge University Press.

Appadurai, Arjun (1996), *Modernity at Large: Cultural Dimensions of Globalization*, Minneapolis: University of Minnesota Press.

Arnaut, Karel (2016), 'Superdiversity: Elements of an Emerging Perspective', in Karel Arnaut, Jan Blommaert, Ben Rampton and Massimiliano Spotti (eds), *Language and Superdiversity*, 49–70, New York: Routledge.

Arnaut, Karel, Martha Sif Karrebæk and Massimiliano Spotti (2017), 'The Poiesis-Infrastructures Nexus and Language Practices in Combinatorial Spaces', in Karel Arnaut, Martha Sif Karrebæk, Massimiliano Spotti, and Jan Blommaert (eds), *Engaging Superdiversity: Recombining Spaces, Times, and Language Practices*, 3–24, Bristol: Multilingual Matters.

Arrow, Kenneth (1951), *Social Choice and Individual Values*, New York: Wiley.

Austin, John L. (1962), *How to Do Things with Words*, Oxford: Oxford University Press.

Backhaus, Gary (2003), 'Husserlian Affinities in Simmel's Later Philosophy of History: The 1918 Essay', *Human Studies*, 26: 223–58.

Bakhtin Mikhail M. (1981), *The Dialogic Imagination*, Austin: University of Texas Press.

Bakhtin Mikhail M. (1986), *Speech Genres and Other Late Essays*, Austin: University of Texas Press.

Baron, Naomi (2008), *Always On: Language in an Online and Mobile World*, Oxford: Oxford University Press.

Bateson, Gregory (1972), *Steps to an Ecology of Mind*, Chicago: University of Chicago Press.

Bauman, Zygmunt (2007), *Liquid Times: Living in an Age of Uncertainty*, Cambridge: Polity.

Bauman, Richard and Charles Briggs (1990), 'Poetics and Performance as Critical Perspectives on Language and Social Life', *Annual Review of Anthropology*, 19: 59–88.

Bauman, Richard and Charles Briggs (2003), *Voices of Modernity: Language Ideology and the Politics of Inequality*, Cambridge: Cambridge University Press.

Becker, Howard (1963), *Outsiders: Studies in the Sociology of Deviance*, New York: Free Press.

Becker, Howard, Blanche Geer, Everett C. Hughes and Anselm Strauss (1961), *Boys in White: Student Culture in Medical School*, Chicago: University of Chicago Press.

Bell, Allan (2016), 'Succeeding Waves: Seeking Sociolinguistic Theory for the Twenty-First Century', in Nikolas Coupland (ed.), *Sociolinguistics: Theoretical Debates*, 391–416, Cambridge: Cambridge University Press.

Bhatt, Rakesh (2001), 'World Englishes', *Annual Review of Anthropology*, 30: 527–50.

Billings, Sabrina (2014), *Language, Globalization and the Making of a Tanzanian Beauty Queen*, Bristol: Multilingual Matters.

Blackledge, Adrian and Angela Creese (2016), '"A Typical Gentleman": Metapragmatic Stereotypes as Systems of Distinction', in Karel Arnaut, Jan Blommaert, Ben Rampton and Massimiliano Spotti (eds), *Language and Superdiversity*, 155–73, New York: Routledge.

Blommaert, Jan, ed. (1999), *Language Ideological Debates*, Berlin: Mouton de Gruyter.

Blommaert, Jan (2001), 'Investigating Narrative Inequality: African Asylum Seekers' Stories in Belgium', *Discourse and Society*, 12 (4): 413–49.

Blommaert, Jan (2005), *Discourse: A Critical Introduction*, Cambridge: Cambridge University Press.

Blommaert, Jan (2006a), 'Language Ideology', in Keith Brown (ed.), *Encyclopaedia of Language and Linguistics*, 2nd edn, Volume 6, 510–22, Oxford: Elsevier.

Blommaert, Jan (2006b), 'Ethnopoetics as Functional Reconstruction: Dell Hymes' Narrative View of the World', *Functions of Language*, 13 (2): 229–49.

Blommaert, Jan (2008a), 'A Market of Accents', *Language Policy*, 8: 243–59.

Blommaert, Jan (2008b), 'Bernstein and Poetics Revisited: Voice, Globalization and Education', *Discourse and Society*, 19 (4): 425–51.

Blommaert, Jan (2008c), *Grassroots Literacy: Writing, Identity and Voice in Central Africa*, London: Routledge.

Blommaert, Jan (2009), 'Language, Asylum and the National Order', *Current Anthropology*, 50 (4): 415–45.

Blommaert, Jan (2010), *The Sociolinguistics of Globalization*, Cambridge: Cambridge University Press.

Blommaert, Jan (2012), 'Supervernaculars and Their Dialects', *Dutch Journal of Applied Linguistics*, 1 (1): 1–14.

Blommaert, Jan (2013), 'From Fieldnotes to Grammar: Artefactual Ideologies of Language and the Micro-Methodology of Linguistics', *Tilburg Papers in Culture Studies* 84. Available online: https://www.tilburguniversity.edu/upload/79420ab5-354f-42fe-b63a-305a5b49aa71_TPCS_84_Blommaert.pdf (accessed 14 June 2017).

Blommaert, Jan (2014), *State Ideology and Language in Tanzania*, Edinburgh: Edinburgh University Press.

Blommaert, Jan (2015a), 'Pierre Bourdieu: Perspectives on Language in Society', in Jan-Ola Östman and Jef Verschueren (eds), *Handbook of Pragmatics 2015*, 1–16, Amsterdam: John Benjamins.

Blommaert, Jan (2015b), 'Language, the Great Diversifier', in Steven Vertovec (ed.), *Routledge International Handbook of Diversity Studies*, 83–90, Abingdon: Routledge.

Blommaert, Jan (2015c), 'Meaning as a Nonlinear Effect: The Birth of Cool', *AILA Review*, 28: 7–27.

Blommaert, Jan (2015d), 'Chronotopes, Scales and Complexity in the Study of Language in Society', *Annual Review of Anthropology*, 44: 105–16.

Blommaert, Jan (2016a), 'Mathematics and its Ideologies: An Anthropologist's Observations', *Tilburg Papers in Culture Studies* 168. Available online: https://www.tilburguniversity.edu/research/ institutes-and-research-groups/babylon/tpcs/item-paper-168-tpcs. htm (accessed 14 June 2017).

Blommaert, Jan (2016b), 'The History of Global Information Networks: Some Notes', *Ctrl+Alt+Dem*. Blog available online: https://alternative-democracy-research.org/2016/04/29/the- history-of-global-information-networks/ (accessed 14 June 2017).

Blommaert, Jan (2016c), 'From Mobility to Complexity in Sociolinguistic Theory and Method', in Nikolas Coupland (ed.), *Sociolinguistics: Theoretical Debates*, 242–59, Cambridge: Cambridge University Press.

Blommaert, Jan (2016d), '"Meeting of Styles" and the Online Infra- structures of Graffiti', *Applied Linguistics Review*, 7 (2): 99–115.

Blommaert, Jan and Ad Backus (2013), 'Superdiverse Repertoires and the Individual', in Ingrid de Saint-Georges and Jean-Jacques Weber (eds), *Multilingualism and Multimodality: Current Challenges for Educational Studies*, 11–32, Rotterdam: Sense Publishers.

Blommaert, Jan and Anna De Fina (2017), 'Chronotopic Identities: On the Timespace Organization of Who We Are', in Anna De Fina, Jeremy Wegner and Didem Ikizoglu (eds), *Diversity and Super-Diversity. Sociocultural Linguistic Perspectives*, 1–15, Washington DC: Georgetown University Press.

Blommaert, Jan and Ben Rampton (2016), 'Language and Superdiversity', in Karel Arnaut, Jan Blommaert, Ben Rampton and Massimiliano Spotti (eds), *Language and Superdiversity*, 21–48, New York: Routledge.

Blommaert, Jan and Piia Varis (2015), 'Enoughness, Accent, and Light Communities: Essays on Contemporary Identities', *Tilburg Papers in Culture Studies* 139. Available online: https://www. tilburguniversity.edu/research/institutes-and-research-groups/ babylon/tpcs/item-paper-139-tpcs.htm (accessed 14 June 2017).

Blommaert, Jan, Sirpa Leppänen, Päivi Pahta and TiinaRäisänen, eds (2012), *Dangerous Multilingualism: Northern Perspectives on Order, Purity and Normality*, Houndmills: Palgrave Macmillan.

Blumer, Herbert (1969), *Symbolic Interactionism: Perspectives and Method*, Englewood Cliffs: Prentice Hall.

Bourdieu, Pierre (1982), *Ce Que Parler Veut Dire: L'Economie des Echanges Linguistiques*, Paris: Fayard.

Bourdieu, Pierre (1984), *Distinction: A Social Critique of the Judgment of Taste*, Cambridge, MA: Harvard University Press.

Bourdieu, Pierre and Jean-Claude Passeron ([1964] 1985), *Les Héritiers: Les Etudiants et la Culture*, Paris: Minuit.

boyd, dana (2011), 'White Flight in Networked Publics? How Race and Class Shaped American Teen Engagement with MySpace and Facebook', in Lisa Nakamura and Peter Chow-White (eds), *Race after the Internet*, 203–22, New York: Routledge.

boyd, dana (2014), *It's Complicated: The Social Lives of Networked Teens*, New Haven: Yale University Press.

Brandehof, Jelke (2014), 'Superdiversity in a Cameroonian Diaspora Community in Ghent: The Social Structure of Superdiverse Networks', MA diss., Tilburg University.

Braudel, Fernand ([1958] 1969), 'Histoire et Sciences Socials: La Longue Durée', in *Ecrits sur l'Histoire*, 41–83, Paris: Flammarion.

Braudel, Fernand (1981), *The Structures of Everyday Life: The Limits of the Possible (Civilization and Capitalism, Vol. 1)*, New York: Harper and Row.

Brevini, Bendetta, Arne Hintz and Patrick McCurdy, eds (2013), *Beyond Wikileaks: Implications for the Future of Communications, Journalism, and Society*, London: Palgrave Macmillan.

Briggs, Charles (1997), 'Notes on a "Confession": On the Construction of Gender, Sexuality, and Violence in an Infanticide Case', *Pragmatics*, 7 (4): 519–46.

Briggs, Charles (2005), 'Communicability, Racial Discourse, and Disease', *Annual Review of Anthropology*, 34: 269–91.

Britain, David (2003), 'Exploring the Importance of the Outlier in Sociolinguistic Dialectology', in David Britain and Jenny Cheshire (eds), *Social Dialectology: In Honour of Peter Trudgill*, 191–208, Amsterdam: John Benjamins.

Britain, David and Jenny Cheshire, eds (2003a), *Social Dialectology: In Honour of Peter Trudgill*, Amsterdam: John Benjamins.

Britain, David and Jenny Cheshire (2003b), 'Introduction', in David Britain and Jenny Cheshire (eds), *Social Dialectology: In Honour of Peter Trudgill*, 1–8, Amsterdam: John Benjamins.

Brown, Penelope and Steven Levinson (1987), *Politeness: Some Universals in Language Use*, Cambridge: Cambridge University Press.

Busch, Brigitta (2015), 'Expanding the Notion of Linguistic Repertoire: On the Concept of *Spracherleben* – The Lived Experience of Language', *Applied Linguistics*, 38 (3): 340–58. Online available: doi:10.1093/applin/amv030 (accessed 14 June 2017).

Carr, E. Sumerson and Michael Lempert (2016), 'Introduction: Pragmatics of Scale', in E. Sumerson Carr and Michael Lempert (eds), *Scale: Discourse and Dimensions of Social Life*, 1–21, Oakland: University of California Press.

Castells, Manuel (1996), *The Rise of the Network Society*, London: Blackwell.

Castells, Manuel (2010), 'Preface to the 2010 Edition', in Manuel Castells (ed.), *The Power of Identity*, 2nd edn, xvii–xxxvi, Oxford: Blackwell.

Charalambous, Costadina, Panayiota Charalambous, Kamran Khan and Ben Rampton (2016), 'Security and Language Policy', *Working Papers in Urban Language and Literacies* 194. Online available: https://www.academia.edu/27503865/WP194_Charalambous_Charalambous_Khan_and_Rampton_2016._Security_and_language_policy (accessed 14 June 2017).

Chomsky, Noam (1965), *Aspects of the Theory of Syntax*, Cambridge, MA: MIT Press.

Chouliaraki, Lilie and Norman Fairclough (1999), *Discourse in Late Modernity: Rethinking Critical Discourse Analysis*, Edinburgh: Edinburgh University Press.

Cicourel, Aaron (1964), *Method and Measurement in Sociology*, New York: Free Press.

Cicourel, Aaron (1967), *The Social Organization of Juvenile Justice*, New York: Wiley.

Cicourel, Aaron (1973), *Cognitive Sociology: Language and Meaning in Social Interaction*, Harmondsworth: Penguin Education.

Cicourel, Aaron (1974), *Theory and Method in a Study of Argentine Fertility*, New York: Wiley.

Collins, Randall (1981), 'On the Microfoundations of Macrosociology', *American Journal of Sociology*, 86 (5): 984–1014.

Collins, James and Richard Blot (2003), *Literacy and Literacies: Texts, Power and Identity*, Cambridge: Cambridge University Press.

Coupland, Nikolas (2007), *Style: Language Variation and Identity*, Cambridge: Cambridge University Press.

Coupland, Nikolas (2015), 'Language, Society and Authenticity: Themes and Perspectives', in Véronique Lacoste, Jakob Leimgruber and Thiemo Breyer (eds), *Indexing Authenticity: Sociolinguistic Perspectives*, 14–39, Berlin: De Gruyter.

Coupland, Nikolas (2016), 'Five Ms for Sociolinguistic Change', in Nikolas Coupland (ed.), *Sociolinguistics: Theoretical Debates*, 433–54, Cambridge: Cambridge University Press.

Coupland, Nikolas and Adam Jaworski (2009), 'Editors' introduction to Part III', in Nikolas Coupland and Adam Jaworski (eds), *The New Sociolinguistics Reader*, 259–64, Houndmills: Palgrave Macmillan.

Creese, Angela and Adrian Blackledge (2010), 'Translanguaging in the Bilingual Classroom: A Pedagogy for Learning and Teaching?' *Modern Language Journal*, 94: 103–15.

Cutler, Celia (2009), 'Yorkville Crossing: White teens, Hip-hop and African American English', in Nikolas Coupland and Adam Jaworski (eds), *The New Sociolinguistics Reader*, 299–310, New York: Palgrave Macmillan.

De Fina, Anna, Deborah Schiffrin and Michael Bamberg (2006),'Introduction', in Anna De Fina, Deborah Schiffrin and Michael Bamberg (eds), *Discourse and Identity*, 1–14, Cambridge: Cambridge University Press.

De Saussure, Ferdinand ([1916] 1960), *Cours de Linguistique Générale*, Paris: Payot.

Deterding, David and Salbrina Sharbawi (2013), *Brunei English: A New Variety in a Multilingual Society*, Dordrecht: Springer.

Du, Caixia (2016), *The Birth of Social Class Online: The Chinese Precariat on the Internet*, PhD Diss., Tilburg University.

Durkheim, Emile ([1897] 1951), *Suicide: A Study in Sociology*, New York: Simon and Schuster.

Durkheim, Emile ([1893] 1967), *De la Division du Travail Social*, Paris: Presses Universitaires de France.

Durkheim, Emile ([1961] 2002), *Moral Education*, Minneola, NY: Dover Publications.

Durkheim, Emile ([1895] 2010), *Les Règles de la Méthode Sociologique*, Paris: Flammarion.

Eckert, Penelope (2008), 'Variation and the Indexical Field', *Journal of Sociolinguistics*, 12: 453–76.

Eckert, Penelope (2012), 'Three Waves of Linguistic Variation: The Emergence of Meaning in the Study of Variation', *Annual Review of Anthropology*, 41: 87–100.

Eckert, Penelope (2015), 'The Trouble with Authenticity', in Véronique Lacoste, Jakob Leimgruber and Thiemo Breyer (eds), *Indexing Authenticity: Sociolinguistic Perspectives*, 43–54, Berlin: De Gruyter.

Eelen, Gino (2001), *A Critique of Politeness Theories*, Manchester: StJerome.

Elbaum, Max (2002), *Revolution in the Air: Sixties Radicals Turn to Lenin, Mao and Che*, London: Verso.

Eriksen, Thomas Hylland (2001), *Tyranny of the Moment*, London: Pluto Press.

Errington, Joseph (1988), *Structure and Style in Javanese*, Philadelphia: University of Pennsylvania Press.

Extra, Guus, Massimiliano Spotti and Piet Van Avermaet, eds (2011), *Language Testing, Migration and Citizenship: Cross-National Perspectives on Integration Regimes*, London: Continuum.

Fabian, Johannes (1983), *Time and the Other: How Anthropology Makes its Object*, New York: Columbia University Press.

Fabian, Johannes (1991), 'Genres in an Emerging Tradition', in *Time and the Work of Anthropology: Critical Essays 1971–1991*, 45–63, Chur: Harwood.

Fairclough, Norman (1992), *Discourse and Social Change*, Cambridge: Polity.

Faudree, Paja (2015), 'Singing for the Dead, On and Off Line: Diversity, Migration and Scale in Mexican *Muertos*Music', *Language and Communication*, 44: 31–43.

Flores, Nelson, Massimiliano Spotti and Ofelia Garcia (2017), 'Conclusion: Moving the Study of Language and Society into the Future', in Ofelia Garcia, Nelson Flores and Massimiliano Spotti (eds), *The Oxford Handbook of Language and Society*, 545–51, New York: Oxford University Press.

Foucault, Michel (1969), *L'Archéologie du Savoir*, Paris: Gallimard.

Foucault, Michel (2003), *Abnormal: Lectures at the Collège de France 1974-1975*, New York: Picador.

Foucault, Michel (2015), *The Punitive Society: Lectures at the Collège de France 1972-1973*, New York: Palgrave Macmillan.

Fox, Susan and Devyani Sharma (2016), 'The Language of London and Londoners', *Working Papers in Urban Language and Literacies* 201. Online available: https://www.academia. edu/29025532/WP201_Fox_and_Sharma_2016._The_language_ of_London_and_Londoners (accessed 14 June 2017).

Gal, Susan (2016), 'Sociolinguistic Differentiation', in Nikolas Coupland (ed.), *Sociolinguistics: Theoretical Debates*, 113–35, Cambridge: Cambridge University Press.

Garfinkel, Harold (1967), *Studies in Ethnomethodology*, Englewood Cliffs: Prentice Hall.

Garfinkel, Harold (2002), *Ethnomethodology's Program: Working Out Durkheim's Aphorism*, edited by Anne Warfield Rawls, Lanham: Rowman and Littlefield.

Gerth, Hans H. and C. Wright Mills (1970), *From Max Weber: Essays in Sociology*, New York: Oxford University Press.

Giddens, Anthony (1976), *New Rules of Sociological Method: A Positive Critique of Interpretive Sociologies*, New York: Basic Books.

Giddens, Anthony (1984), *The Constitution of Society: Outline of the Theory of Structuration*, Cambridge: Polity Press.

Giles, Howard, Nikolas Coupland and Justine Coupland (1991), *Contexts of Accommodation: Developments in Applied Sociolinguistics*, Cambridge: Cambridge University Press.

Glaser, Barney and Anselm Strauss ([1967] 1999), *The Discovery of Grounded Theory: Strategies for Qualitative Research*, New Brunswick: Aldine Transactions.

Goebel, Zane (2013), 'Common Ground and Conviviality: Indonesians Doing Togetherness in Japan', *Multilingual Margins*, 2 (1): 46–66.

Goebel, Zane (2015), *Language and Superdiversity: Indonesians Knowledging Home and Abroad*, Oxford: Oxford University Press.

Goffman, Erving (1959), *The Presentation of Self in Everyday Life*, New York: Doubleday.

Goffman, Erving (1961), *Encounters: Two Studies in the Sociology of Interaction*, New York: Bobbs-Merrill.

Goffman, Erving (1967), *Interaction Ritual: Essays on Face-to-Face Behavior*, New York: Doubleday.

Goffman, Erving (1971), *Relations in Public: Microstudies of the Public Order*, New York: Basic Books.

Goffman, Erving (1974), *Frame Analysis: An Essay on the Organization of Experience*, New York: Harper and Row.

Goffman, Erving (1981), *Forms of Talk*, Philadelphia: University of Pennsylvania Press.

Goodwin, Charles (1994), 'Professional Vision', *American Anthropologist*, 96: 606–33.

Goodwin, Charles (2007), 'Participation, Stance and Affect in the Organization of Practice', *Discourse and Society*, 18 (1): 53–73.

Goodwin, Charles and Marjorie Harness Goodwin (2004), 'Participation', in Alessandro Duranti (ed.), *A Companion to Linguistic Anthropology*, 222–44, Malden: Blackwell.

Graeber, David (2009), *Direct Action: An Ethnography*, Edinburgh: AK Press.

Graeber, David (2015), *The Utopia of Rules: On Technology, Stupidity, and the Secret Joys of Bureaucracy*, Brooklyn: Melville House.

Green, Donald and Ian Shapiro (1994), *Pathologies of Rational Choice: A Critique of Applications in Political Science*, New Haven: Yale University Press.

Grice, H. Paul (1975), 'Logic and Conversation', in Peter Cole and J. Morgan (eds), *Syntax and Semantics, Vol. III: Speech Acts*, 41–58, New York: Academic Press.

Gumperz, John (1968), 'The Speech Community', in David Sills (ed.), *International Encyclopaedia of the Social Sciences*, 381–86, New York: Macmillan and Free Press.

Gumperz, John (1982), *Discourse Strategies*, Cambridge: Cambridge University Press.

Habermas, Jurgen (1984), *The Theory of Communicative Action,* Vol. 1, Boston: Beacon Press.

Halliday, Michael (1978), *Language as Social Semitic*, London: Edward Arnold.

Hanell, Linnea and Linus Salö (2015), '"That's weird, my ob-gyn said the exact opposite!" Discourse and Knowledge in an Online Discussion Forum Thread for Expecting Parents', *Tilburg Papers in Cultural Studies* 125. Online available: https://www.tilburguniversity.edu/upload/dc6b8024-c200-4dbd-8bdb-bd684aa636c0_TPCS_125_Hanell-Salo.pdf (accessed 15 June 2017).

Harris, Roxy (2006), *New Ethnicities and Language Use*, London: Palgrave Macmillan.

Haviland, John (1989), '"Sure, sure": Evidence and Affect', *Text*, 9: 27–68.

Haviland, John (2003),'Ideologies of Language: Some Reflections on Language and US Law', *American Anthropologist*, 105: 764–74.

Heath, Joseph (2015),'Methodological Individualism', in Edward Zalta (ed.), *The Stanford Encyclopedia of Philosophy* (Spring 2015 Edition). Online available: https://plato.stanford.edu/archives/spr2015/entries/methodological-individualism (accessed 15 June 2017).

Heller, Monica (2010), 'Language as Resource in the Globalized New Economy', in Nikolas Coupland (ed.), *The Handbook of Language and Globalization*, 349–65, Oxford: Wiley-Blackwell.

Heynders, Odile (2016), *Writers as Public Intellectuals: Literature, Celebrity, Democracy*, London: Palgrave Macmillan.

Hill, Jane (2001), 'Mock Spanish, Covert Racism and the (Leaky) Boundary between Public and Private Spheres', in Susan Gal and Kathryn Woolard (eds), *Languages and Publics: The Making of Authority*, 83–102, Manchester: StJerome.

Hobsbawm, Eric (1987), *The Age of Empire, 1875-1914*, London: Weidenfeld and Nicholson.

Hobsbawm, Eric (2008), *Globalisation, Democracy and Terrorism*, London: Abacus.

Holton, Judith (2008), 'Grounded Theory as a General Research Methodology', *Grounded Theory Review*, 7 (4). Online available: http://groundedtheoryreview.com/2008/06/30/grounded-theory-as-a-general-research-methodology/ (accessed 15 June 2017)

Hughes, Everett C. ([1971] 2009), *The Sociological Eye: Selected Papers*, New Brunswick: Transaction Publishers.

Hymes, Dell, ed. (1964), *Language in Culture and Society: A Reader in Linguistics and Anthropology*, New York: Harper and Row.

Hymes, Dell (1966), 'Two Types of Linguistic Relativity (with examples from Amerindian ethnography)', in William Bright (ed.), *Sociolinguistics: Proceedings of the UCLA Sociolinguistics Conference, 1964*, 114–67, The Hague: Mouton.

Hymes, Dell (1980), 'Speech and Language: On the Origins and Foundations of Inequality among Speakers', in Dell Hymes, *Language in Education: Ethnolinguistic Essays*, 19–61, Washington, DC: Center for Applied Linguistics.

Hymes, Dell (1981), *In Vain I Tried to Tell You: Essays in Native American Ethnopoetics*, Philadelphia: University of Pennsylvania Press.

Hymes, Dell ([1972] 1986), 'Models of the Interaction of Language and Social Life', in John Gumperz and Dell Hymes (eds), *Directions in Sociolinguistics: The Ethnography of Communication*, 35–71, London: Basil Blackwell.

Hymes, Dell (1992), 'The Concept of Communicative Competence Revisited', in Martin Pütz (ed.), *Thirty Years of Linguistic Evolution*, 31–57, Amsterdam and Philadelphia: JohnBenjamins.

Hymes, Dell (1996), *Ethnography, Linguistics, Narrative Inequality: Toward An Understanding Of Voice*, London: Taylor & Francis.

Irvine, Judith (2001), 'Genres of Conquest: From Literature to Science in Colonial African Linguistics', in Herbert Knoblauch and Helga Kotthoff (eds), *Verbal Art across Cultures*, 63–89, Tübingen: Gunter Narr.

Irvine, Judith and Susan Gal (2000), 'Language Ideology and Linguistic Differentiation', in Paul Kroskrity (ed.), *Regimes of Language*, 35–83, Santa Fe: SAR Press.

Jacquemet, Marco (2015), 'Asylum and Superdiversity: The Search for Denotational Accuracy during Asylum Hearings', *Language and Communication*, 44: 72–81.

Jaffe, Alexandra (1999), *Ideologies in Action: Language Politics on Corsica*, Berlin: Mouton de Gruyter.

Jaworski, Adam and Crispin Thurlow (2010), 'Language and the Globalizing Habitus of Tourism: Toward a Sociolinguistics of Fleeting Relationships', in Nikolas Coupland (ed.) *The Handbook of Language and Globalization*, 255–86, Oxford: Wiley-Blackwell.

Jewitt, Carey (2013), 'Multimodal Methods for Researching Digital Technologies', in Sara Price, Carey Jewitt and Barry Brown (eds), *The Sage Handbook of Digital Technology Research*, 250–65, Los Angeles: Sage.

Johnstone, Barbara (2010), 'Indexing the Local', in Nikolas Coupland (ed.), *The Handbook of Language and Globalization*, 386–405, Oxford: Wiley-Blackwell.

Jones, Graham (2014), 'Reported Speech as an Authentication Tactic in Computer-Mediated Communication', in Véronique Lacoste, Jakob Leimgruber and Thiemo Breier (eds), *Indexing Authenticity: Sociolinguistic Perspectives*, 188–208, Berlin: De Gruyter.

Jørgensen, Jens Normann (2008), *Languaging: Nine Years of Poly-Lingual Development of Young Turkish-Danish Grade School Students*, Copenhagen: University of Copenhagen Faculty of Humanities.

Jørgensen, Jens Normann, Martha Sif Karrebæk, Lian Malai Madsen and Janus Spindler Møller (2016), 'Polylanguaging in Superdiversity', in Karel Arnaut, Jan Blommaert, Ben Rampton and Massimiliano Spotti (eds), *Language and Superdiversity*, 137–54, New York: Routledge.

Juffermans, Kasper (2015), *Local Languaging: Literacy and Multilingualism in a West African Society*, Bristol: Multilingual Matters.

Kailoglou, Lefteris (2015), 'Being More Alternative and Less Brit-Pop: The Quest for Originality in Three Urban Styles in Athens', in Véronique Lacoste, Jakob Leimgruber and Thiemo Breyer (eds), *Indexing Authenticity: Sociolinguistic Perspectives*, 78–96, Berlin: De Gruyter.

Katz, Jerrold J. (1972), *Semantic Theory*, New York: Harper and Row.

Kelly-Holmes, Helen (2010), 'Languages and Global Marketing', in Nikolas Coupland (ed.), *The Handbook of Language and Globalization*, 475–92, Oxford: Wiley-Blackwell.

Kerswill, Paul (2003), 'Dialect Leveling and Geographical Diffusion in British English', in David Britain and Jenny Cheshire (eds), *Social Dialectology: In Honour of Peter Trudgill*, 223–43, Amsterdam: John Benjamins.

Khan, Kamran (2017), 'Citizenship, Securitization and Suspicion in UK ESOL Policy', in Karel Arnaut, Martha Sif Karrebæk, Massimiliano Spotti and Jan Blommaert (eds), *Engaging Superdiversity: Recombining Spaces, Times and Language Practices*, 303–20, Bristol: Multilingual Matters.

Kothari, Rita (2011), 'English *Aajkal*: Hinglish in Hindi Cinema', in Rita Kothari and Rupert Snell (eds), *Chutnefying English: The Phenomenon of Hinglish*, 112–27, New Delhi: Penguin Books India.

Kothari, Rita and Rupert Snell, eds (2011), *Chutnefying English: The Phenomenon of Hinglish*, New Delhi: Penguin Books India.

Kress, Gunther (2003), *Literacy in the New Media Age*, London: Routledge.

Kroskrity, Paul, Bambi Schieffelin and Kathryn Woolard, eds (1992), Language Ideologies, Special Issue of *Pragmatics*, 2 (3): 235–453.

Kytölä, Samu (2013), *Multilingual Language Use and Metapragmatic Reflexivity in Finnish Internet Football Forums: A Study in the Sociolinguistics of Globalization*, PhD Diss., University of Jyväskylä.

Kytölä, Samu and Elina Westinen (2015), '"Chocolate munch-
ing wanabee rapper, you're out": A Finnish Footballer's Twitter
Writing as the Focus of Metapragmatic Debates', *Tilburg Papers
in Culture Studies* 128. Online available: https://www.tilburgu-
niversity.edu/upload/6f479b83-f64d-48d4-bb6c-988e15935c71_
TPCS_128_Kytola-Westinen.pdf (accessed 15 June 2017).

Laitin, David (1992), *Language Repertoires and State Construction
in Africa*, Cambridge: Cambridge University Press.

Lave, Jean and Etienne Wenger (1991), *Situated Learning:
Legitimate Peripheral Participation*, Cambridge: Cambridge
University Press.

Le Page, Robert B. and Andrée Tabouret-Keller (1985), *Acts of
Identity: Creole-Based Approaches to Language and Ethnicity*,
Cambridge: Cambridge University Press.

Leppänen, Sirpa (2007), 'Youth Language in Media Contexts:
Insights into the Function of English in Finland', *World
Englishes*, 26 (2): 149–69.

Leppänen, Sirpa and Ari Elo (2016), 'Buffalaxing the Other:
Superdiversity in Action on YouTube', in Karel Arnaut, Jan
Blommaert, Ben Rampton and Massimiliano Spotti (eds),
Language and Superdiversity, 110–36, New York: Routledge.

Leppänen, Sirpa and Sajja Peuronen (2012), 'Multilingualism on the
Internet', in Marilyn Martin-Jones, Adrian Blackledge and Angela
Creese (eds), *Handbook of Multilingualism*, 384–402, London:
Routledge.

Leppänen, Sirpa, Elina Westinen and Samu Kytölä, eds (2017),
Social Media Discourse: (Dis)identifications and Diversities,
London: Routledge.

Li Kunming, Massimiliano Spotti and Sjaak Kroon (2014), 'An
E-Ethnography of *Baifumei* on the Baidu Tieba: Investigating
an Emerging Economy of Identification Online,' *Tilburg
Papers in Culture Studies* 120. Available online: https://www.
tilburguniversity.edu/upload/c7982626-e1a6-40a8-9334-
9fba945ac568_TPCS_120_Kunming-Spotti-Kroon.pdf (accessed
15 June 2017).

Lukes, Steven (1973). *Emile Durkheim, His Life and Work: A
Historical and Critical Study*, Harmondsworth: Penguin.

Madsen, Lian Malai (2015), *Fighters, Girls, and Other Identities:
Sociolinguistics in a Martial Arts Club*, Bristol: Multilingual
Matters.

Madsen, Lian Malai (2017), 'Social Status Relations and Enregisterment: Integrated Speech in Copenhagen', in Karel Arnaut, Martha Sif Karrebæk and Massimiliano Spotti, and Jan Blommaert (eds), *Engaging Superdiversity: Recombining Spaces, Times, and Language Practices*, 147–69, Bristol: Multilingual Matters.

Madsen, Lian Malai, Martha Sif Karrebæk and Janus Spindler Møller, eds (2015), *Everyday Languaging: Collaborative Research on the Language Use of Children and Youth*, Berlin: De Guyter.

Maly, Ico (2016), 'How Did Trump Get This Far? Explaining Trumps Message', *Diggit Magazine* 17 October 2106. Available online: https://www.diggitmagazine.com/articles/how-did-trump-get-far (accessed 15 June 2017).

Maly, Ico and Piia Varis (2015), 'The 21st-Century Hipster: On Micro-Populations in Times of Superdiversity', *European Journal of Cultural Studies*, 19 (6): 1–17.

Maryns, Katrijn (2006), *The Asylum Speaker: Language in the Belgian Asylum Procedure*, London: Routledge.

McCaughey, Martha and Michael Ayers, eds (2003), *Cyberactivism: Online Activism in Theory and Practice*, New York: Routledge.

Meeuwis, Michael and Jan Blommaert (1994), 'The "Markedness Model" and the Absence of Society: Remarks on Codeswitching', *Multilingua*, 13 (4): 387–423.

Mehan, Hugh (1996), 'The Construction of an LD Student: A Case Study in the Politics of Representation', in Michael Silverstein and Greg Urban (eds), *Natural Histories of Discourse*, 253–76, Chicago: University of Chicago Press.

Mendoza-Denton, Norma (2015), 'Gangs on YouTube: Localism, Spanish/English Variation, and Music Fandom', *Working Papers in Urban Language and Literacies* 157. Available online: https://www.academia.edu/11599619/WP157_Mendoza-Denton_2015._Gangs_on_YouTube_Localism_Spanish_English_variation_and_music_fandom (accessed 15 June 2017).

Miller, Vincent (2008), 'New Media, Networking and Phatic Culture', *Convergence*, 14: 387–400.

Mills, C. Wright (1951), *White Collar: The American Middle Classes*, New York: Oxford University Press.

Mills, C. Wright ([1959] 2000), *The Sociological Imagination*, New York: Oxford University Press.

Møller, Janus Spindler (2017), '"You Black Black": Polycentric Norms for the Use of Terms Associated with Ethnicity', in Karel Arnaut, Martha Sif Karrebæk, Massimiliano Spotti, and Jan Blommaert (eds), *Engaging Superdiversity: Recombining Spaces, Times and Language Practices*, 123–46, Bristol: Multilingual Matters.

Moore, Robert E. (2017), '"Taking up Speech" in an Endangered Language: Bilingual Discourse in a Heritage Language Classroom', in Karel Arnaut, Martha Sif Karrebæk, Massimiliano Spotti, and Jan Blommaert (eds), *Engaging Superdiversity: Recombining Spaces, Times, and Language Practices*, 65–89, Bristol: Multilingual Matters.

Mufwene, Salikoko (2010), 'Globalization, Global English, and World English(es): Myths and Facts', in Nikolas Coupland (ed.) *The Handbook of Language and Globalization*, 31–55, Oxford: Wiley-Blackwell.

Myers-Scotton, Carol (1993), *Social Motivations for Codeswitching: Evidence from Africa*, Oxford: Clarendon Press.

Myrdal, Gunnar (1944), *An American Dilemma: The Negro Problem and Modern Democracy*, New York: Harper.

Nemcova, Monika (2016), 'Rethinking Integration: Superdiversity in the Networks of Transnational Individuals', *Tilburg Papers in Culture Studies* 167. Available online: https://www.tilburguniversity.edu/upload/d1833428-a654-4a72-aefc-be19edeea82d_TPCS_167_Nemcova.pdf (accessed 15 June 2017).

Page, Ruth (2012), *Stories and Social Media: Identities and Interaction*, London: Routledge.

Pariser, Eli (2011), *The Filter Bubble: What the Internet is Hiding from You*, New York: Penguin Press.

Park, Joseph and Lionel Wee (2012), *Markets of English: Linguistic Capital and Language Policy in a Globalizing World*, London: Routledge.

Parkin, David (2016), 'From Multilingual Classification to Translingual Ontology: A Turning Point', in Karel Arnaut, Jan Blommaert, Ben Rampton and Massimiliano Spotti (eds), *Language and Superdiversity*, 71–88, New York: Routledge.

Parsons, Talcott (1937), *The Structure of Social Action*, New York: McGraw Hill.

Parsons, Talcott (1964), *Social Structure and Personality*, New York: Free Press.

Parsons, Talcott (2007), *American Society: A Theory of the Societal Community*, Boulder: Paradigm Press.

Pennycook, Alastair (2007), *Global Englishes and Transcultural Flows*, London: Routledge.

Pennycook, Alastair (2010), *Language as a Local Practice*, London: Routledge.

Perez-Milans, Miguel (2017), 'Reflexivity and Social Change in Applied Linguistics', *AILA Review*, 29: 1–14.

Philips, Susan (2000), 'Constructing a Tongan Nation-State through Language Ideology in the Courtroom', in Paul Kroskrity (ed.), *Regimes of Language*, 229–57, Santa Fe: SAR Press.

Rampton, Ben (1995), *Crossing: Language and Ethnicity among Adolescents*, London: Longman.

Rampton, Ben (2001), 'Critique in Interaction', *Critique of Anthropology*, 21 (1): 83–107.

Rampton, Ben (2006), *Language in Late Modernity: Interactions in an Urban School*, Cambridge: Cambridge University Press.

Rampton, Ben (2009), 'Speech Community and Beyond', in Nikolas Coupland and Adam Jaworski (eds), *The New Sociolinguistics Reader*, 694–713, New York: Palgrave Macmillan.

Rampton, Ben (2011), 'From "Multi-Ethnic Adolescent Heteroglossia" to "Contemporary Urban Vernaculars"', *Language and Communication*, 31: 276–94.

Rampton, Ben (2016a), 'Drilling Down to the Grain in Superdiversity', in Karel Arnaut, Jan Blommaert, Ben Rampton and Massimiliano Spotti (eds), *Language and Superdiversity*, 91–109, New York: Routledge.

Rampton, Ben (2016b), 'Foucault, Gumperz and Governmentality: Interaction, Power and Subjectivity in the Twenty-First Century', in Nikolas Coupland (ed.), *Sociolinguistics: Theoretical Debates*, 303–28, Cambridge: Cambridge University Press.

Read, Donald (1992), *The Power of News: The History of Reuters*, Oxford: Oxford University Press.

Roberts, Celia (2016), 'Translating Global Experience into Institutional Models of Competency: Linguistic Inequality in the Job Interview', in Karel Arnaut, Jan Blommaert, Ben Rampton and Massimiliano Spotti (eds), *Language and Superdiversity*, 237–60, New York: Routledge.

Rodgers, Dennis and Bruce O'Neill (2012), 'Infrastructural Violence: Introduction to the Special Issue', *Ethnography*, 13 (4): 401–12.

Rymes, Betsy (2014), *Communicating Beyond Language: Everyday Encounters with Diversity*, New York: Routledge.

Schegloff, Emanuel A., Gail Jefferson and Harvey Sacks (1977), 'The Preference for Self-Correction in the Organisation of Repair in Conversation', *Language*, 53: 361–82.

Schieffelin, Bambi and Elinor Ochs, eds (1986), *Language Socialization across Cultures*, Cambridge: Cambridge University Press.

Scott, Mary (2013), *A Chronicle of Learning: Voicing the Text*, PhD Diss., Tilburg University.

Seargeant, Philip (2009), *The Idea of English in Japan: Ideology and the Evolution of a Global Language*, Bristol: Multilingual Matters.

Seargeant, Philip and Caroline Tagg, eds (2014), *The Language of Social Media: Identity and Community on the Internet*, Houndmills: Palgrave Macmillan.

Searle, John (1969), *Speech Acts: An Essay in the Philosophy of Language*, Cambridge: Cambridge University Press.

Sierra, Sylvia (2016), 'Playing Out Loud: Videogame References as Resources in Friend Interaction for Managing Frames, Epistemics, and Group Identity', *Language in Society*, 45: 217–45.

Silverstein, Michael (1977), 'Cultural Prerequisites to Grammatical Analysis', in Muriel Saville-Troike (ed.), *Linguistics and Anthropology* (GURT 1977), 139–51, Washington DC: Georgetown University Press.

Silverstein, Michael (1979), 'Language Structure and Linguistic Ideology', in Paul Clyne, William Hanks and Carol Hofbauer (eds), *The Elements: A Parasession on Linguistic Units and Levels*, 193–247, Chicago: Chicago Linguistic Society.

Silverstein, Michael (1985), 'The Pragmatic Poetry of Prose: Parallelism, Repetition and Cohesive Structure in the Time Course of Dyadic Conversation', in Deborah Schiffrin (ed.), *Meaning, Form and Use in Context*, 181–99, Washington DC: Georgetown University Press.

Silverstein, Michael (1992), 'The Uses and Utility of Ideology: Some Reflections', in Paul Kroskrity, Bambi Schieffelin and Kathryn Woolard (eds), *Language Ideologies*, Special Issue of *Pragmatics*, 2 (3): 311–23.

Silverstein, Michael (1996), 'Monoglot "Standard" in America: Standardization and Metaphors of Linguistic Hegemony', in Donald Brenneis and Ronald Macaulay (eds), *The Matrix of*

Language: Contemporary Linguistic Anthropology, 284–306, Boulder: Westview Press.

Silverstein, Michael (1997), 'The Improvisational Performance of Culture in Realtime Discursive Practice', in Keith Sawyer (ed.), *Creativity in Performance*, 265–312, Greenwich, CT: Ablex.

Silverstein, Michael (1998), 'Contemporary Transformations of Local Linguistic Communities', *Annual Review of Anthropology*, 27: 401–26.

Silverstein, Michael (2003), 'Indexical Order and the Dialectics of Social Life', *Language and Communication*, 23 (3–4): 193–229.

Silverstein, Michael (2004), '"Cultural" Concepts and the Language-Culture Nexus', *Current Anthropology*, 45: 621–52.

Silverstein, Michael (2005), 'Axes of Evals: Token Versus Type Interdiscursivity', *Journal of Linguistic Anthropology*, 15 (1): 6–22.

Silverstein, Michael (2006), 'Old Wine, New Ethnographic Lexicography', *Annual Review of Anthropology*, 35: 481–96.

Silverstein, Michael (2015), 'The Race from Place: Dialect Eradication vs. the Linguistic "Authenticity" of *Terroir*', in Véronique Lacoste, Jakob Leimgruber and Thiemo Breyer (eds), *Indexing Authenticity: Sociolinguistic Perspectives*, 159–87, Berlin: De Gruyter.

Silverstein, Michael (2016), 'The "Push" of *Lautgesetze*, the "Pull" of Enregisterment', in Nikolas Coupland (ed.), *Sociolinguistics: Theoretical Debates*, 37–67, Cambridge: Cambridge University Press.

Silverstein, Michael and Greg Urban, eds (1996), *Natural Histories of Discourse*, Chicago: University of Chicago Press.

Simmel, Georg (1950), *The Sociology of Georg Simmel,* edited by Kurt H. Wolff, Glencoe: The Free Press.

Spotti, Massimiliano (2016), 'Sociolinguistic Shibboleths at the Institutional Gate: Language, Origin, and the Construction of Asylum Seekers' Identities', in Karel Arnaut, Jan Blommaert, Ben Rampton and Massimiliano Spotti (eds), *Language and Superdiversity*, 261–78, New York: Routledge.

Stæhr, Andreas (2017), 'Languaging on the Facebook Wall: Normativity on Facebook', in Karel Arnaut, Martha Sif Karrebæk, Massimiliano Spotti, and Jan Blommaert (eds), *Engaging Superdiversity: Recombining Spaces, Times, and Language Practices*, 170–95, Bristol: Multilingual Matters.

Standing, Guy (2011), *The Precariat: The New Dangerous Class*,
London: Bloomsbury.

Strauss, Anselm (1993), *Continual Permutations of Action*,
New Brunswick: Transaction Publishers.

Tagliamonte, Sali (2015), 'So Sick or So Cool? The Language of
Youth on the Internet', *Language in Society*, 45: 1–32.

Tall, Serigne Mansour (2004), 'Senegalese Émigrés: New Information
and Communication Technologies', *Review of African Political
Economy*, 99: 31–48.

Thaler, Richard H. (2015), *Misbehaving: The Making of Behavioral
Economics*, New York: Norton and Company.

Thompson, Edward P. (1968), *The Making of the English Working
Class*, London: Victor Gollancz.

Thompson, John B. (1984), *Studies in the Theory of Ideology*,
Cambridge: Polity Press.

Thompson, John B. (1990), *Ideology and Modern Culture*,
Cambridge: Polity Press.

Toma, Catalina (2016), 'Online Dating', in Charles Berger and
Michael Roloff (eds), *The International Encyclopaedia of
Interpersonal Communication*, 1–5, New York: Wiley.

Tufekci, Zeynep (2015), 'Algorithmic Harms beyond Facebook and
Google: Emergent Challenges of Computational Agency', *Journal
on Telecommunications and High Technology Law*, 13: 203–17.

Van der Aa, Jef (2012), *Ethnographic Monitoring: Language,
Narrative and Voice in a Caribbean Classroom*, PhD Diss.,
Tilburg University.

Van Nuenen, Tom (2016), *Scripted Journeys: A Study of Interfaced
Travel Writing*, PhD Diss., Tilburg University.

Varis, Piia and Jan Blommaert (2013), 'Conviviality and Collectives
on Social Media: Virality, Memes, and New Social Structures',
Multilingual Margins, 2 (1): 31–45.

Varis, Piia and Tom van Nuenen (2017), 'The Internet, Language,
and Virtual Interactions', in Ofelia Garcia, Nelson Flores and
Massimiliano Spotti (eds), *The Oxford Handbook of Language
and Society*, 473–88, New York: Oxford University Press.

Varis, Piia and Xuan Wang (2011), 'Superdiversity on the Internet: A
Case from China', *Diversities*, 13 (2): 71–83.

Velghe, Fie (2013), '"Hallo, hoe gaan dit, wat maakjy?" Phatic
Communication, the Mobile Phone and Coping Strategies in a
South African Context', *Multilingual Margins*, 2 (1): 10–30.

Verschueren, Jef (1999), *Understanding Pragmatics*, London: Arnold.

Wang, Xuan (2015), 'Inauthentic Authenticity: Semiotic Design and Globalization in the Margins of China', *Semiotica*, 203: 227–48.

Wang, Xuan, Kasper Juffermans and Caixia Du (2012), 'Harmony as Language Policy in China: An Internet Perspective', *Tilburg Papers in Culture Study* 35. Available online: https://www.tilburguniversity.edu/upload/6ed0ff66-891c-4cbf-bf2f-0abfa633aa61_tpcs%20paper35.pdf (accessed 15 June 2017).

Wang, Xuan, Massimiliano Spotti, Kasper Juffermans, Leonie Cornips, Sjaak Kroon and Jan Blommaert (2014), 'Globalization in the Margins: Towards a Re-Evaluation of Language and Mobility', *Applied Linguistics Review*, 5 (1): 23–44.

Watts, Richard (2003), 'Why *Fuude* is not "Food" and *Tschëgge* is not "Check": A New Look at the Actuation Problem', in David Britain and Jenny Cheshire (eds), *Social Dialectology: In Honour of Peter Trudgill*, 115–29, Amsterdam: John Benjamins.

Williams, Glyn (1992), *Sociolinguistics: A Sociological Critique*, London: Longman.

Wortham, Stanton and Angela Reyes (2015), *Discourse Analysis Beyond the Speech Event*, New York: Routledge.

Woydack, Johanna (2017), 'Superdiversity and a London Multilingual Call Center', in Karel Arnaut, Martha Sif Karrebæk, Massimiliano Spotti, and Jan Blommaert (eds), *Engaging Superdiversity: Recombining Spaces, Times, and Language Practices*, 220–47, Bristol: Multilingual Matters.

Yang Peidong, Lijun Tang and Xuan Wang (2015), '*Diaosi* as Infrapolitics: Scatological Tropes, Identity-Making and Cultural Intimacy on China's Internet', *Media, Culture and Society*, 37 (2): 197–214.

INDEX